Radical Freedom

Jay Cradeur
www.jaycradeur.com

CONTENTS

DEDICATION

First I dedicate this book to my parents. Throughout all of my rebellion and trailblazing, highs and lows, I always knew I was loved. This served as the perfect lesson for me as a parent. I also dedicate this book to the writers that have inspired me, in particular, Ernest Hemingway, Carlos Castaneda, Charles Bukowski and Stuart Wilde. This book is also dedicated to my children, Brookes, Sarah, Michael and Paulina. I hope this serves as a reminder for them to speak their minds, question everything, and develop their own philosophy of life. I dedicate this to all the women in my life who have taught me hard life lessons. I have learned painfully, heartbrokenly, lovingly, sternly, gently, and often with great care for my well-being. I dedicate this book to the men, my brothers in arms, the guys who have been with me through thick and thin. You know who you are. What a ride it has been. May it continue ever more. And finally, to Led Zeppelin. When I first heard Stairway to Heaven as a teenager, my world was rocked. I have often said Led Zeppelin is my one true love that after 40 years has never lets me down. And with that, I am complete.

PREFACE

"Your only obligation in any lifetime is to be true to yourself."

— Richard Bach

The year was 2000. I was sitting in my living room in the Old Rectory in Cromhall, England. I was in front of our fireplace, cross-legged, meditating, letting my mind relax and get still. Suddenly a vision appeared. There I was, on an African plain, sitting on the solid clay earth. Ahead of me was a circle of warriors in their most celebratory garb. They were facing inward, toward the chief of the tribe. I knew instinctively to get up and walk toward the chief. He was strong, full of life, with a radiant energy and palpable inner peace. As I entered into the circle, the chief locked into my eyes with a fierce demeanor. I knew to hold his gaze as I approached. I arrived and stopped about one foot in front of him, his intense eyes looking right through me. Then he burst into laughter, and all the brothers in the circle also began to bellow. I had arrived home.

After some time had passed, he asked me if I had a question for him, for certainly, I had met my spirit guide. I asked him what I was to do with the rest of my life. He told me, "Show people how to live a simple life."

INTRODUCTION

"The only way to deal with an unfree world is to become so absolutely free that your very existence is an act of rebellion."

— Albert Camus

This book is written for those of us who harbor a glimmer of hope for real freedom, who understand the importance of the space between our ears, who are committed to establishing a powerful and supportive paradigm. There is a way of being that frees us of the bonds of this earthly existence, and allows us to experience the exuberance of a life fully lived. This book serves as a long spindly finger pointing the direction, just beyond the horizon, where something rare and beautiful lives.

Recently, I was sitting on Bangtao Beach in the Phuket area of Thailand. It is a long beach, with white sand, warm water, and just a handful of people, as it was the low season in late August. I had to ask myself, why did it take me so long to realize a dream that I had been carrying around for over 15 years? Ever since I met a traveling mystic in 1998, and ever since I had the vision with the African warrior, I knew in my heart that traveling and writing and sharing were all I wanted to do. And yet, for 15 years I resisted, I found excuses, I struggled, I took bad advice, and ultimately I suffered. Why is it so hard to be exactly who we know ourselves to be? Why is it so difficult to set our own self free?

Social conditioning is, without a doubt, the single greatest obstacle to you being you, and me being me. Each and every time I had made a big decision in my life to do something new and different and authentically me, I was met with vehement objections. There are some of my close

1

family and friends who are always supportive, but the vast majority is simply opposed to change and anything that challenges the status quo. Therefore, a big part of pursuing and achieving any real freedom is to pick your friends and associates carefully. It is ridiculously difficult to break away from the pack without a support team. If you were to pick your all-star support team, the people who would empower you rather than tear you down, the people who are also expressing their own freedom to be exactly who they are, who would you select? Write those names down and connect with those folks. They are gold to you, and your hard work and results will be gold to them in return.

Religious conditioning is a close second when it comes to inhibitors of your personal freedom. I am not here to bash religion. I realize that for millions of people, religion is an essential and integral part of life. I do, however, contend that many religious tenets have the exact opposite effect of fostering personal freedom. Quite contrarily, having everyone believe the same thing, and act in the same way, appears to be the goal. This is driving the train away from freethinking, personal liberation and pure self-expression. If you were raised in a religious environment, as I was, it can be challenging to unearth your own authentic feelings and thoughts, and then be willing to take action upon them despite how those actions will be construed by other members of the tribe.

Sex is an area where it is easy to see how social and religious conditioning work to impede us from pursuing and exploring our freedoms and our pleasures. During my life, I have had many opportunities to engage with a beautiful partner, but something stopped me. There was just too much social and religious conditioning swimming around in my head. It makes no sense to blame anyone. In the end, I stopped me. Following my self-imposed stoppage, I then felt embarrassed, emasculated, and shamed. It wasn't until I took decisive action to deal with these feelings and track them back to their source that I began to feel sexually free and relaxed, and inspired to engage without shame and guilt. Having spent so much time with men in a sacred circle, I know this is a common issue. Our gut says one thing, but then we think, and reason, and before we know it, the opportunity for reciprocal touch and intimacy has passed. Rather than breathe in our primal masculine energy, we turn into SNAGs (sensitive new age guys) and walk away limp and frustrated.

Another arena where we see similar roadblocks is in the area of drugs. Some drugs can provide profound shifts in consciousness. This is beyond dispute. Why alcohol and tobacco are legal, while a drug like ecstasy is illegal, defies logic. Yet that is the system we have here in America. This is acceptable. This is not. It makes me wonder who is in charge, and who is making these decisions? What is the end game? Who benefits and who loses? This book is an invitation to live life by your own standards, to create your own authority and live your life true to no one but you.

Radical freedom refers to every action we take in life. This ultimate freedom has been for me, the ultimate goal of my life. We work hard to survive, and then take our enjoyments where we can. Achieving radical freedom turns every moment into a present moment. It keep us in the now, not lost in the past nor hopelessly romanticizing the future. Who are you really? Have you ever had the courage to ask yourself? I suggest it takes courage because your answer, in most cases, will be a far cry from the person you are now. But it will be that discontent that will drive you into focused action to turn it around and work hard to get into alignment, not just with the universe, but with who you and the universe know yourself to be. How perfect is that!

I assert there are four basic freedoms every human being desires: financial freedom, time freedom, geographical freedom, and spiritual freedom. All of this can be summed up in the expression "Radical Freedom." What is demanded to achieve these freedoms is a clear understanding of what is required, the courage to take the appropriate action, and a healthy does of grace.

This book is structured the way I like books to be structured. I don't generally care for laborious information-laden books. My writing style is to the point and not too flowery. My motto is, "Less words, more meaning!" I like to pick up a book, turn to any page and read something of value and hold on to a few words that I can ponder. I also love to read quotes, so each step leads with a quote, for they often simplify a complex concept, making it palatable and digestible. The steps are in an order of sorts, as much as they can be. Personal growth is not a linear progression, and each person has his or her own history coloring the process. I suggest you start at the beginning and see how that feels, or you may just look at the table of contents and pick a topic that hits home for you, or my favorite, just run your fingers over the edge of the book, and open it up to whatever page spirit selects for you.

Anyone who lives a life of radical freedom will tell you that you already have a life of radical freedom. There is nothing to pursue, for you already have it. The journey, therefore, is to eliminate all the misunderstandings and wrong thinking that has temporarily blocked you from the ultimate and natural experience of radical freedom. Richard Rose refers to this as the Reverse Vector approach. Right now, you can experience an awakening to your true nature and feel how natural it is to be exactly who you are devoid of the ego and all its clever trappings. The question this book attempts to answer is how do you arrive back home where you have always been. It is one thing to understand radical freedom as a concept, but quite another thing altogether to live in the space of radical freedom as a daily practice.

There are a few basic tenets I have lived by and will share with you in this book. You will read some of these themes over and over throughout the steps. First, I assert that you and I and everyone else are living a hero's quest. We are all amazing, overcoming obstacles, persevering, and learning and growing each and every day. We all have a story and it is incumbent upon us all to learn our story and share our story. You are unique, you have rare gifts, and you must discover those gifts and share them. I believe life is an experience we can flow with, rather than confront and bend to our will. There is a mode of being that allows for ease and grace rather than struggle and a battle. From this place of being, one can live in a constant mode of exuberance. Exuberance, full of energy, fired up, unhinged and fully surrendered. To be a fully integrated human being, you must know yourself, both the light side, the good stuff, as well as the dark side, the energies we don't want to acknowledge. In those dark energies lie tremendous power you need access to in order to be a fully integrated human being. And finally, we are all heading in the direction of an awakening, a realization that you and I are not separate from, but are rather one with. We are slowly trudging toward the realization that our dual nature is an illusion, and that oneness is reality. When living in this awareness, there is no fear, no loneliness, and no doubt. This is the place of radical freedom, and like it or not, we are all heading there. This book will serve for many as a short cut to the inevitable.

This book is part personal journey, part observation, part instruction, and mostly it is my calling to share a few things I have picked up along the path. Each one of us comes to this present moment with a unique and varied perspective on just what this journey called life is all about, and how to make the best of it and achieve whatever it is we want to achieve. Radical freedom is our birthright. It is my observation that the great majority of us want this freedom, and will take rather remarkable steps to achieve it. This book is for those of you who want to step out of your comfort zone, that want to jump off the cliff and figure it out on the way down, that want to burn the boats so you only have two options, move forward or die. Blessed may your journey be.

The 44 Steps

Step 1

Begin with the End in Mind

"I know you're out there. I can feel you now. I know that you're afraid. You're afraid of us. You're afraid of change. I don't know the future. I didn't come here to tell you how this is going to end. I came here to tell you how it's going to begin. I'm going to hang up this phone, and then I'm going to show these people what you don't want then to see. I'm going to show them a world… without you. A world without rules and controls, without border or boundaries. A world where anything is possible. Where we go from there is a choice I leave to you."

—Neo from the movie, The Matrix

The Matrix ranks as one of my top 5 movies of all time (*The Matrix, The Godfather, Apocalypse Now Redux, Man on Fire, Revolver*). These are the last words spoken in the movie, and they present a clear vision. Not only is this a perfect example of a vision, but it is a vision about radical freedom. It is a vision that works on many levels, but at its most basic, it expresses the desire to be free of outside influences, free from societal influences, free from government influences, and free to exist in a world of unlimited possibility. What is your vision?

For many, having lived most of our lives in service to others, to our parents, to a spouse, to our children, to our jobs, we don't have much experience voicing our own needs and wants. This step is an opportunity for you to do just that. Most people don't know what they want. This is a sad but true fact. Having been swept up in the rushing rapids of life, who has time to stop, assess our lives, and create a vision for the future? Instead, life becomes a day-to-day grind with no end in sight. Unlike you, most people don't take the time to look inside and see what it is they really want, and learn how to go out and get it.

What could be more wonderful than to talk about what you want? Yet there is something inside many of us that stops us from feeling that feeling. We get afraid; we think we can't really do it. We have been disappointed before. It won't really happen. These are the limiting beliefs of which we must let go. These limiting beliefs may have supported us in the past, but they don't any longer. You must remain fixed on your vision. It is the power and clarity of your vision that will drive you, and support you to establish the discipline, the work ethic, the resiliency, the dogged determination to get it done, and turn your vision into a reality. When the going gets tough, and it will, it will be your vision, like a beacon of light in stormy waters, that will empower you to keep moving forward and not give up.

No one is going to tell you it is easy. Well, at least I won't! Transformation is not always pretty. However, when you get to the other side, and you look back, and you see a life well lived, you will breathe easy knowing you didn't sit back. No, you placed your stake in the ground and passionately pursued your vision. I can't think of a more admirable and honorable pursuit.

Last Spring, just around the end of March, I started to have this crazy idea. Turns out it was not so crazy. The idea at the time was to move to Playa Del Carmen, Mexico (one hour south of Cancun) for the winter. I had just taken on a new role as a coach with an Internet marketing company. It soon became clear that as long as I lived in a spot with a decent Internet connection, I could work and live anywhere. "Have MacBook will travel!"

As I look back, this seems like a perfectly logical response to my desire to live in a warm environment, to see the world, and to begin the empty nest phase of my life (my youngest would be going to university in August). In retrospect, this was an absolutely brilliant choice. But it did not turn out exactly as I had anticipated. No…far from it. Actually it was about 10,437 miles far from it. How did this happen?

I was sitting in my Sebastopol, CA home one day about a month after my initial idea to venture out into the wild blue. I was sitting on my favorite sofa doing some channel surfing when I stumbled upon an Anthony Bourdain show on CNN. This is a prime example of synchronicity, a sure sign something good and magical is happening. The show started with our inimitable host, bohemian extraordinaire, Mr. Bourdain stating: "I remember the first moment I realized I had been living my life in black and white. It was like discovering a color I never knew had existed before. A whole new crayon box full of colors. That was it for me. From then on there was no putting the pieces back together, no going home. Things were different now. Asia had ruined me from my old life." That hooked me. The rest of the show reeled me in. Good bye Playa, hello Thailand.

One thing I particularly remember from the TV program was a woman in a cowboy hat who served stewed pork leg over rice. It is moments like this that reinforce my choice to be a carnivore. I have often thought about becoming a vegetarian. I did it for about a year in college. But in the end with all things considered, I love meat. My body seems to crave protein in the form of animal flesh. I've read the books and seen the movies about how animals are processed, and while there are compelling arguments, my body works best this way. So.... when I saw this woman, and her pork, that pretty well closed the deal. I would go to Chiang Mai, Thailand, and find that woman and eat that pork. This was my mission.

The thing I want to emphasize is the importance of having a clearly visualized goal. In this case, it was easy. I saw the woman, I saw the pork, I saw everything I needed to see about Thailand, to create a vision of my life, a vision that continued to inform my actions to make this trip happen. I am writing to you from a hotel room in Chiang Mai. Last night, I ate the pork, and I will do it again many times on this trip. I continue to learn that if I can clearly and vividly visualize something, and then take action, what I see in my mind's eye will become a reality in the physical world. That's a valuable lesson. We all have this particular type of magic living within us. What do you see for yourself? Think big. You will have more fun that way!

If you don't know where you are going, any road will take you there. If you know where you are going, you will most likely take the road less traveled (Thank you Robert Frost!). It is important that you spend some time envisioning what you want. Begin with the end in mind. This is vitally important. This is step one. What do you want? This step is an opportunity for you to create a vision for yourself. As much as you can, picture your answers to the following questions in your mind. This will help to make it more real. The more energy you can put into this vision, the more your actions will be in alignment with the realization of your vision.

Assignment:

Start by finding some time, about 30 minutes, in which you won't be disturbed. Close the door, turn OFF your cell phone, and put it someplace outside of the room in which you will be doing this process.

Sit down and bring yourself to the present moment. This is best done by closing your eyes and focusing on your breath. Do this for at least 5 minutes. Then open your eyes and read through the questions and take as much time as necessary to write down the answers. Use pen and paper and actually handwrite the answers. Oftentimes, as you write, new and possibly more refined answers will appear.

This is a rare opportunity to take some time for yourself and get some clarity about what you really and truly want in your life. This vision process will be freeing. Let go. Let your imagination run with it. Surrender these next few minutes to the process.

Following are a series of questions. All you need to do is feel for your answers and then write them down. Keep these answers and refer to them anytime you are questioning your direction in life.

Let's start with the broadest question first, and then go deeper with the details.

If you could live the life of your dreams, and you could realize everything you want without any repercussions, what would your perfect standard day be? Not a special day. What would you want everyday of your life to look like? Lets just sit with that for a minute. What would your perfect day look like?

Now I am going to help you to stretch beyond where you might be looking right now.

Let's start with money. Assume you have no limitations. There is no budget. For this process, assume you have enough money for everything you need.

Health. How do you see yourself during your perfect day? Even though you may not be healthy now, see yourself experiencing your perfect day in the exact level of health you desire.

Where do you live? This is a mighty big world. Expand beyond your current location. Where would you really and truly want to live?

People. Who is in your life? Perhaps there are some people in your life that you'd rather not be in your life. For your perfect day, who is in and who is out? And what type of new people might you want in your life?

What would your house look like? Imagine your house as your temple, your sanctuary. How many rooms? What does the kitchen look like? How about your bedroom, and your office? What kind of bathroom do you have, and what about the shower and tub? How many showerheads and how many jets? How many can fit in your bathtub?

Here is a good one. What time do you want to wake up each day? What time do you want to go to sleep? Be sure to get your 8 hours of sleep.

What does your morning look like? What is your morning ritual? What do you eat for breakfast? Who prepares your breakfast? Is it you, or has somebody else prepared it and your food is waiting for you?

If you have children, how do you take care of them and their needs? Do you have help? Do you want to do it all on your own?

Now let's move a little later in the day. What do you do up till noon? If you have work, what is the work you do that brings you the greatest joy?

During your work, what do you actually spend your time doing, really?

And then lunch. Do you dine alone, or are there people you'd like to share your lunch with. Remember this is your everyday, normal, average, and still amazing day.

If you have lunch with people, what are they like? The people you hang out with, your friends, what are they like?

And how about your relationship? Are you in an intimate relationship? Who are you with? What do you do together? If you have a family, what is family time like?

Let's move towards dinner, what do you eat? What time do you eat? Again, who do you eat dinner with? Is it a family meal? Do you enjoy sharing your meal with friends? And what are you talking about at the table? Or do you like to dine alone? Is your food healthy, or decadent, or both?

Now it is time to approach the end of the day. Who are you with? What do you do? Can you see your ideal end of day ritual, the one that puts you to sleep with the greatest ease and joy? What are you thinking just before you fall to sleep?

*****

When you have completed the vision process, summarize your day by writing down the top 5, or predominate, activities. Look at this list in the morning when you wake up and in the evening before you go to sleep. Make it real.

Step 2

Curiosity, Desire and the Damnedest Discontent

"A most astounding phenomenon has happened to us; we have had an experience which makes Love, fame, rank, ambition, wealth, look like thirty cents; and we begin to wonder passionately, "What is truth?" The Universe has tumbled about our ears like a house of cards, and we have tumbled too. Yet this ruin is like the opening of the Gates of Heaven! Here is a tremendous problem, and there is something within us which ravins for its solution."

—Aleister Crowley

There are three things you must have if you are going to make the journey toward radical freedom. Don't worry; you already have all these things living within you. You may not have been aware of them until now, nor how they brilliantly work together to drive your personal growth. Without each one of them, you won't make an impact, and you will return to the status quo of your life. These three states work together, in harmony, to create an ongoing transformation. Curiosity opens the door. Desire is that feeling you get when you want what you see. Discontent over what you lack is the bitter pill, which does not feel good, yet creates the energy for you to transform as necessary to be and do and have what you want. Once you see how the mechanism works, it is simply wash, rinse and repeat as you naturally expand your horizons in your pursuit for what is real and true and free.

I have already used the word transformation several times. Having spent many of my weekends in transformational workshops, I would like to share with you my observation of transformation. Transformation is not change. When someone is transformed, they are not changed. No, they are, in fact, different. Transformation requires some part of you to die, usually a part of you that is no longer of value to you. Then in its place, something new and different appears. In other words, when something dies, there is then an energetic gap, or space, which works like a vacuum, and calls for something to fill the void. I have had the privilege of seeing these transformations hundreds of times. Each time I marvel at the mysterious nature of spirit and the human desire to grow and expand and awaken.

My observation is that we are all born curious by nature. When I watch children, they are always exploring, smelling and tasting things. With unbounded energy, they experience as much life as they possibly can. Over time, for some, a feeling of reticence settles in. The curiosity button has been pushed for the last time. Or for others, ego has convinced you that you know all you need to know, so you don't have to deal with the uncertainty and the unknown that comes with curiosity. The ego does not like the unknown at all. No thank you. The ego will convince you that this physical life is all there is, all this spiritual talk is mumbo jumbo, and the idea of achieving radical freedom is just a pipe dream. Instead, let's turn on the television and take a nap!

Still, for many of us, and certainly anyone who is reading this book, there is a spark of awareness that there is something more, something profound, something even beyond words that is the real reason we are here in the physical dimension. We are the curious ones. We have had a few experiences, which point to a greater truth, and a more fully integrated way of being. Once you uncork the genie, you can't put it back in the bottle. It is a sad sight to see someone who has uncorked the genie, and then try to pretend they did not do it. You may try to go back to sleep, but you can never really and truly go back. You jumped, and sooner or later, you will begin to free-fall, as is your destiny.

This curiosity will lead us to pursue experiences. Many quench their curiosity by engaging with other like-minded individuals, or attending workshops, or traveling, or reading books. For the curious mind, the world is an amusement park full of cotton candy, clowns and roller coaster rides. Curiosity exposes us to more of the world, and to all the many different interpretations of life. Curiosity opens us up to a whole new world of perception, one that crosses the barrier of the physical world. Chakras, energy fields, and the etheric body start to become realities, rather than concepts read about in a book.

When we delve into these experiences, it is natural to have desires. When we see something we don't understand, we have a natural desire to understand. When I see someone who is living a life of radical freedom, it is natural to desire the same thing. I have been blessed to hang out with some remarkable individuals during my life, and for a great part of that time, I desired to be more like them and less like me. I saw something that was pure, and good, and often powerful, and my desire to obtain what I saw and experienced, was palpable. In fact, it was seeing these qualities in those individuals, and desiring them for myself that created such discontent. My life's mission became to grow and expand and wake up to their same realities.

Discontent is hard. It is the damnedest thing. By its very nature, you can not be content with discontent. We need it, and yet it feels like pain and suffering and wanting and confusion, and regret. Discontent features ego at its most effective. Ego, as we have discussed, does not like the unknown. So when you desire something you really don't know how to achieve, your ego will try to dissuade you from moving forward. Unfortunately for the ego, and fortunately for you, once the genie has been let out of the bottle, she is not going back in. The only way to assuage the discontent is to move toward that which you desire. The pain leads to action, which leads you to that which you desire. Once you have been through this cycle a few times, you will recognize it and embrace the discontent, for you understand there is something wonderful about to happen.

*"Look, if you ever want to discover anything of importance," he said with
great seriousness, "you've got to get this Pollyanna crap out of your heads.
People think they can indulge in whatever whim overpowers them at the
moment, and that somehow this 'spontaneity' is going to transform them
into a wonderful spiritual creature that God just can't resist loving. This is
nonsense."*

—Richard Rose

The road to mastery is strewn with discontent. You may follow your
bliss all you like, but unless you do the hard work, your bliss will be
short-lived and elusive. One cannot become a master without going
through the pain. There is no going around it. Until one stops trying
all the intricate ways we have at our disposal to navigate around the
hard work, little, if anything, is accomplished. Rather than embrace
our natural state, we run, really run, in the opposite direction. We are
like Forrest Gump. "Run, Forrest, run!" Rather than sacrifice in place,
we hightail it to the next pleasurable experience. Our lives are a series
of state changes, of ways to avoid the wisdom and knowledge that
comes from pain and suffering and discontent. The key is to remember
it is a cycle, and there is a light on the other side, and just when you
want to give up, there is the golden nugget of awakening and wisdom
waiting for you.

The glorious aspect about this, and that which leads to exuberance,
is that as you achieve what you desire, it is as if a whole new world
opens up. This sparks your curiosity, which sparks new desires, which
leads to more discontent, which then leads to another whole new realm
of experience. Wash, rinse and repeat. This is how it works. I am sorry
to burst your bubble. Life is not non-stop bliss. As Richard Rose says,
get the Pollyanna crap out of your heads. There is no way around
the pain that is necessary to grow. Anyone who tells you different is
either lying to you, or worse, trying to sell you something for their
personal gain. Accept the rules, use the rules, and you will reduce your
suffering and strife. It will still hurt at times, but this knowledge will
put you in the best mindset to get the most out of your life.

Assignment:

Write down the 3 most challenging times of your life, and the lessons you learned from each one. Demonstrate how the cycle presented in this step has worked in your life.

Step 3

Embrace Your Hero's Quest

"To seek freedom is the only driving force I know. Freedom to fly off into that infinity out there. Freedom to dissolve; to lift off; to be like the flame of a candle, which, in spite of being up against the light of a billion stars, remains intact, because it never pretended to be more than what it is: a mere candle."

— Carlos Castaneda

Begin right now to shift the context of your life story. Many walk the Earth as a victim. It is time now to become the author of your life, and to see it as a hero's quest. This is a shift in context that must happen. If you already see your life as a mighty trek toward the Holy Grail, well done. However, most have lost the plot and life keeps plodding and beating them down and sucking the vital energy of self-fulfillment right out of them. Don't pretend to be less than you are. This step invites you to become the Picasso of your life, with a glorious palate of colors at your fingertips and a marvelously white canvas laid out in front of you.

You have had some experiences through your life, amazing tales of difficulty and strife, which you overcame, pushed through to the other side, and exited as a conquering hero. Can you see it? You may have experienced a life threatening illness. You may have lived with an abuser, and survived to become a beacon of hope for others. Or, like me, you may have just endured the hurtful words of a 6th grade girl, and used that experience to go deep within yourself and discover who you really are. We all have a story of power and inspiration. What is your story? The assignment for this step is to write down your story, and shift the context of the narrative to that of a hero's quest. When I undertook this process several years ago, here is the story I wrote.

<u>The Story of Jay</u>

I was a rambunctious child. You know how boys are. King of the world. I enjoyed playing, riding my bike, playing sports. I was a good swimmer when I was 10 years old. I came in second place in all of California in the 50-yard freestyle. You get the picture. I was a rambunctious and naïve little boy who was king of his castle.

Something happened when I was in sixth grade. In all my work with people in my events, you'd be surprised at how many hurtful events happen to us in and around sixth grade. I attended a Catholic School. We had a daily class called Religion, and day after day, I learned about God, Jesus, Mary, and the Holy Ghost. I also learned about all the rules and how not to go to hell.

My teacher in 6th grade was a man who volunteered to teach at the school. His name was Mr. Martin. He was a stern disciplinarian. The boys in the class were afraid of his index finger. When he got angry with us, he'd poke us in the center of the chest and it looked like it hurt. I never got the iron finger treatment, but some of my friends did, and it left a nice red mark. No doubt, today he'd be locked up for child abuse. But back then, getting your knuckles whacked with a ruler, or Mr. Martin's finger treatment, were just challenges we had to adjust to and accept.

The other character I must introduce is Lila. She was my friend. We had been going to the same school for 6 years. She hung out with the cool girls in the class, and there was a large group of them that spent time together. Then one day, it happened. It probably won't seem like much to you, but this thing that happened, it impacted my life more than any other event.

So you get the picture? There I was, doing nothing but being happy, living life and playing with my friends. I was also avoiding the iron finger of death. I was comfortable with this group of children that have mostly all been together for 6 years. Then Lila, the leader of the girls group, she says these two words.

But wait, I have to explain something to you. You all know me as Jay. That is what everyone calls me. But my legal name is Jerry, so that is what all the teachers called me, so that is what some of the kids called me as well. Ok, now we are ready for the two words…

Two freakin' words. Well, actually its three words, but sounds like two. Here it is. The words she spoke to her girlfriends and my guy friends.

"Jerry's conceited."

Bam. My world changed.

"Jerry's conceited."

As a result, my whole way of being changed. Everything changed. From those two words, all the girls treated me different. And since the girls and the boys were starting to get interested in each other, the boys started to treat me different too. I was ostracized and treated like a pariah.

I lost all my confidence. I walked on eggshells. I developed hay fever. I crashed. I became a pariah, really. The only way I could deal with it was to go in the opposite direction, and project an air of inferiority, and become the kid who was quiet, kept to himself, and tried to establish just a few friendships. I still remember the kids saying I had an "inferiority complex," and I was OK with that. It was so much better than what had happened. At least I could get some pity, which was better than disdain.

In Grail mythology, this seminal event in a boy's life is called the fisher king wound, which impacts men and women throughout their lives.

"The whole Grail castle is in serious trouble because the Fisher King is wounded. The myth tells us that years before, early in his adolescence, when he was out wandering around in the woods doing his knight errantry, the Fisher King came to a camp. All the people of the camp were gone, but there was a salmon roasting on a spit. He was hungry, there was a salmon roasting over the fire, and he took a bit of it to eat. He found that the salmon was very hot. After burning his fingers on it he dropped the salmon and put his fingers into his mouth to assuage the burn. In so doing he got a bit of the salmon into his mouth. This is the Fisher King wound and gives its name to the ruler of much of our modern psychology. Modern suffering man is the heir to this psychological event which took place culturally some eight hundred years ago.

Most western men are Fisher Kings. Every boy has naively blundered into something that is too big for him. He proceeds halfway through his masculine development and then drops it as being too hot. Often a certain bitterness arises, because, like the Fisher King, he can neither live with the new consciousness he has touched nor can he entirely drop it.

Every adolescent receive his Fisher King wound. He would never proceed into consciousness if it were not so."

—He by Robert Johnson

And for the women:

"I doubt if there is a woman in the world who has not had to mutely stand by as she watched a man agonize over his Fisher King aspect. She may be the one who notices, even before the man himself is aware of it, that there is suffering and a haunting sense of injury and incompleteness in him. A man suffering in this way is often driven to do idiotic things to cure the wound and ease the desperation he feels. Usually he seeks an unconscious solution outside of himself, complaining about

this work, his marriage, or his place in the world.

The Fisher King is carried about in his litter, groaning, crying in his suffering. There is no respite for him – except when he is fishing. This is to say that the wound, which represents consciousness, is bearable only when the wounded is doing his inner work, proceeding with the task of consciousness which was inadvertently started with the wound in his youth."

—She by Robert Johnson.

As you can imagine, for most of my life, I had a real issue with abandonment. When people left me, it hurt. And I'd plead, and write letters, and buy gifts, and basically do everything I could so she (any woman) wouldn't leave me. All of this made her more certain of her decision to leave, and she was gone. However this forced me to go inwards to discover the real source of the pain so I could marshal forward in my life once again with confidence and joy. Let's jump ahead and you'll see how those words of Lila's led me to a profound moment of my life, all of which has led me to be here with you today.

Let's fast forward to the late 1990s at which time my wife and I did well for ourselves. We were both in sales, and we found a product to sell that earned us a tidy sum. We decided to take some time off, and take the kids and live in England for a year. We put a bunch of stuff in storage. We packed more stuff up to be shipped to Europe. We went over in July 2000. It took us a couple of months to find a place, and we settled on an old rectory, actually called the Old Rectory, in a little village called Cromhall in the Southwest part of England, near Bath and Bristol.

Toward the end of the year, we received a phone call from a friend who told us all of our money, which we had placed in the hands of a trusted associate, was gone. We trusted the wrong guy. We had nothing. We would have to head back to America and get back to work, which is exactly what we did.

Upon our return, I started to work again, trying to find the same rhythm I had before the Europe trip. But things were different. My priorities had shifted. Money just wasn't all that important. Exploring my inner worlds had taken over as job #1. During that time, my wife was also going through some profound changes, and decided she did not want to be married any longer. We had been together 14 years at the time, so this came as quite a shock. And even though I did not think about 6th grade Lila at the time, this stirred up all of those traumatic feelings of abandonment and loss.

This whole period of time I have come to call my Van Gogh period. I had no money. This was my bottom. You know how people in recovery talk about their bottom? This was absolutely my bottom. I had no place to go, and no money to pay for a place to live in the same town as my wife and daughter. So I sent an email out to all of my male friends, and one wonderful man offered me a room in his home for a nominal fee. It was over an hour drive away from my 8-year-old daughter, but it was the best I could do. Humbled Jay now began to feel some gratitude.

During that time, I was leading a weekly men's group, doing weekend events, selling advertising on a truck, and driving from Oakland to Sonoma County twice a week, once to attend a weekly sweat lodge, and another to spend time with my daughter. My wife and I were still intimate from time to time, which I guess gave me hope that things might turn around.

The sweat lodge was an important part of my life. I attended this weekly ritual for about a year. I spent one month as the fire master, which meant I would arrive 4 hours ahead of the actual start time of the lodge, and set the wood and the rocks, and then start the fire and maintain it until it was time to begin the lodge. Then I'd pick the rocks out of the fire, brush off the ash, and slide them into the lodge for placement in the center.

A sweat lodge, if you have never been in one, is all about purifying yourself. It is a physical and spiritual purification. It is one of the most honest places you can be. Approximately 20 men would crawl into the lodge and sweat, pray, and tell the truth about what was important for us. It pushes your buttons. Stifling and painful heat will do that. Small cramped space and darkness and confronting the unknown trigger all sorts of fears. It is not uncommon for men to leave mid way through the ritual. It is intense.

And still for me, it felt like home. I'd sit inside and look at the red-hot rocks glowing in the darkness. The main leader of the ritual often put cedar on the stones and the smoke would fill the lodge. My favorite scent was sweet grass, which, when it touched the red stones, emitted a glorious smoke. It was a slice of heaven, akin, I imagine, to being in a womb.

The other thing that was happening for me during this time was a voracious appetite for books and knowledge. I had, and still do have, an indefatigable hunger for OPE (other people's experiences): Castaneda. McKenna, Thoreau, Vernon Howard, Richard Rose, Adi Da, Whitman, Hemingway, Bukowski, Osho, Wilde and Krishnamurti. And out of this reading, and everything being so different in my life, I was having some unusual experiences. For example, one day I felt I had lost my mind, as I would see my face in everything: other faces, clouds, cars, cats, you name it, I was there. And synchronicities were compounding. I would think about somebody and they would call. Or I would sit in a café, and think about the back of someone's neck, and then they'd scratch it. I was also having some extremely rich and vibrant visions during my meditation of all sorts of things. I would travel to what has been called the astral plane, a place of beauty and wisdom, which always helped out a bit with the puzzle I was trying to put together. There was a fire in my belly that was burning out of control

So, now we are at the big day. Little did I know what would happen this day. But this was the day I gained something extremely valuable. It started out with an emergency. I didn't have any money to pay the cell phone bill and the phone company was going to cut it off that day. That meant my wife, son, daughter, and I wouldn't have a phone. This was a big deal!! I grabbed my male pride, what little of it there was left, and called a friend to see if he would meet with me. He agreed. I felt my chances of success were better if I asked him for money in person. Then I had to drive over to Mill Valley to meet with my friend and hopefully get some money for the phone bill. I stopped on my way at a cheese steak shop on Lakeshore Drive in Oakland.

I had just ordered my cheesesteak sandwich and I was waiting. My phone rang (I guess ATT had not cut it off yet!). It was my wife, calling to tell me she no longer wanted to be lovers. She said, "I need a break." And here was the first miracle. The first miracle of the day was that I was A-OK with it. No pain. No fear. Something had shifted as I accepted her request. Finally, the curse of 6th grade Lila had lifted. For the first time, I felt good about being alone with myself. But I still had bigger fish to fry on this magical day.

It was over the bridge to my friend's house, and then I was off to Sebastopol to attend my weekly sweat lodge. I ate the cheesesteak and drove over to Mill Valley and met with my friend. He was so awesome, and asked me to tell him what I needed. I said $1,000 and he said "OK." I got a check and headed out of there toward Sonoma County. I now had miracle #2 under my belt. (Have you ever seen *Good Fellas*? The movie? I felt like the Ray Liotta character at the end of the film when he is driving around making all those deals, looking to the sky and seeing a helicopter after him, trying to remain calm, but having to surrender to the energy of the day.)

By now it was only 1:00 and the sweat lodge wasn't until 6:00. I don't know why I was drawn to the ocean that day, but I was. I do love spending time at the ocean, so off I headed to Salmon Creek Beach for what turned out to be quite a memorable day at the ocean. I arrived at the parking lot at Salmon Creek Beach just north of Bodega Bay. Driving down to the end of the parking lot near the bathrooms, I got out of my car, proceeded down the pathway, and greeted the river where it meets the ocean. I walked along the beach for 10 or so minutes, heading north toward a smaller beach separated by a group of rocks. I sat down and something unusual and beautiful happened. I vanished. Jay disappeared.

For the next two hours, I was transported out of normal waking reality into a space I have come to call Everything/Nothing. I immediately noticed how the waves looked different. Rather than waves, they were effervescent puffs of universal power. Each wave brought with it a swirly, misty, heavenly burst of energy. I was present, and yet, somehow, I was not. I remember being in awe of the beauty of it all, the waves, the clouds, the sky, the birds, all performing in concert. Remarkably, I was also intensely aware that I was the waves, the clouds, the sky and the birds. I was everything that ever has and ever will exist.

I have since come to understand that this experience is called Samadhi. What is Samadhi? It has been described as a non-dualistic state of consciousness in which the consciousness of the experiencing subject (me) becomes one with the experienced object (everything else), and in which the mind becomes still, one-pointed or concentrated while the person remains conscious. That about sums it up.

To say that I vanished must sound quite bizarre. But that is how it felt. That is how it was and is. Think of it like you are a dandelion, when all of its parts get blown into the air to expand out into the universe. I was blatantly aware that something magical was happening to me. Yet, it wasn't magic. It seemed so natural at the time. Imagine, being at the beach, looking at the ocean, and knowing in your soul, in your being, in every atom of your body, that you are, in fact, the waves, the clouds, the sky and the birds. How remarkable! For two hours, I was treated to the most glorious show on earth, exposed to the greatest mystery in this dimension, and trusted with the only truth that withstands scrutiny.

I have come to know that the path I had been on was one of negation. Over 45 years of living, I had come to understand I was not any of the titles I had been assigned through a lifetime. This process of burning, this decimation of me, left me with nothing to hold on to that was mine, that was, in fact, me. With all that gone, I realized right there on the beach that I am truly nothing. And I am everything.

So I watched the waves for a while. I watched the sky and clouds for even longer. It didn't matter where I set my vision; the feeling in my body was one of utter and complete freedom. I had nothing to protect. I had nothing to lose. I had not a thought in my head. I had not a care in the world. I laughed and I cried. Deep in my soul, I knew this was the greatest single moment of my life. This was it! This was what Don Juan in the Castaneda books referred to as "stopping the world." My eyes welled up with tears. I was once again complete, as if I had returned to the womb.

I learned that day that my real satisfaction, the deep joy, lives in the very real knowing that everything is perfect just as it is: You, me, the world. If everything stayed just the same, and nothing "improved," I would still be content and grateful and alive and not wanting.

*****

And so that is my hero's journey. That is how I now see the history of my life. Transforming your life's story to that of Hero will transform your present moment experience. Your life as a victim of circumstance leaves you at the effect of everything around you. As creator of your life, as hero of your quest, you are back in the driver's seat, full of life, vision, and an unwavering desire to be free. So, Hero, now that I have shared my story, let's say we move on to the topic of developing your own unique voice and Rock the Casbah!

Assignment:

This is important. Take some time to write down your life story in the format of a hero's quest similar to what I just shared with you. What have you overcome, and what have you learned? When has life kicked you in the teeth, and you got up and kicked back? Be sure to include the vision you are moving toward realizing. It is valuable to know who you are in the proper context of hero rather than victim.

Step 4

Raise Your Voice

"Let us be silent, that we may hear the whisper of God."

— Ralph Waldo Emerson

When I read this quote, I think of the whisper as my inner voice, my inner knowing, and my inner wisdom. Contrarily, I think of my ego as a loud voice often speaking as if through a bullhorn. It is the whisper that guides my life. It is the whisper that speaks from a place of unconditional acceptance. It is the whisper that will inform me that I have a voice and I have something to say. And, the wee little voice says, "You damned well better say it!"

"You must not let your life run in the ordinary way; do something that nobody else has done, something that will dazzle the world. Show that God's creative principle works in you."

— Paramahansa Yogananda

You have something to say. You have something to share that will dazzle your world. But perhaps you are afraid to say it or do it. What will everyone think of me? Why should I risk it? What's the point? The point is that by speaking your truth, by expressing yourself, by risking the criticism of others, you will strengthen your energy body like few other activities. Speaking about something makes it real. Taking the thoughts out of your head, and putting them out into the world, not only makes those thoughts real, but it makes you real.

The only thing that truly interests others is the uniqueness of you and how you express that uniqueness. They are not interested in how or what you know about this or that, but rather what you think or feel about this or that. Isn't it true that the only thing you or I have that is authentically our own is our unique self-expression, our voice, our imprimatur, in whatever form it takes? Everything else is more of the same. This is an invitation to step out of the shadows and take the risk and express yourself.

This whisper of which Emerson speaks does not necessarily have to be expressed as a voice, or the written word. You have a gift, many gifts; something you do better than most other people, and it is the expression of that gift that is your voice. For me, for example, I thrive in group events, workshops, in which I can engage with others in a safe and intimate environment. I don't have to think about anything; rather, my thoughts and words flow very naturally. And from the feedback I hear from others, my words strike at the heart of the matter, and some form of transformation takes place. This is one of my gifts. What is your gift? What is your voice? What does your voice say? What are some things that you naturally do better than most other people. You don't have to think about it. It is authentic and free flowing.

There are certain activities that will raise your energy, and others that will blast holes in your energy body. We want to focus on the energy building activities, and minimize the deleterious ones. Finding your voice, and expressing it, is high on the energy building scale. Full self-expression requires a courage most are unwilling to embrace. Why? What are you afraid of? I assert we all have a healthy dose of a specific fear, which I will call the "whispering of the neighbors." What will my friends think? How will I be judged? How will I be perceived? What will anyone who disagrees with me think? How will this impact my friendships? In short, what will the neighbors think? All of which I have to ask you, why do you care? What is more important to you? Is being a cog in a system that rewards the status quo what you want? Or do you want radical freedom? Why choose to be a prisoner of your own mind, when you have an opportunity to break free and experience a life of wonder, vigor, potency and vibrancy.

That really is the question, isn't it? What do you choose, freedom or slavery? What does your spirit long for, self-expression or self-censorship? I can't overemphasize this point. You must choose your own rebellion, your own transformation, and your own right to create your life rather than have all the forces that are impinging on you create a life for you. Fly like an eagle or join the herd of sheep?

"The two most important days in your life are the day you were born and the day you find out why?"

— Mark Twain

The world is thirsty for new voices, new forms of self-expression, people who have found their gift and are willing to express it freely for all to hear. Radical freedom demands of you to be exactly who you are, and part of the ticket price of admission is exploring who you are, discovering your strengths and your gifts, and then courageously and willingly sharing with the world. There are few things more heartbreaking than a gift that goes dormant. Raise your voice. Speak up. Say and do what you came here to say and do. We are all waiting to hear you and your uniqueness. Dance, sister, dance!

Assignment:

Take 10 minutes in silence and ask yourself, what is my gift for the world? As an answer arrives, write it down. Come up with at least 3 gifts. Take another 10 minutes, and write your findings into a mission statement using the following format.

1. I _____ am here on planet Earth to share my gifts. I will discover and learn and practice all the ways I can express my gift of _____.

2. I _____ am here on planet Earth to share my gifts. I will discover and learn and practice all the ways I can express my gift of _____.

3. I _____ am here on planet Earth to share my gifts. I will discover and learn and practice all the ways I can express my gift of _____.

Step 5

Self Authority

"Not I, nor anyone else can travel that road for you.
You must travel it by yourself.
It is not far. It is within reach.
Perhaps you have been on it since you were born, and did not know.
Perhaps it is everywhere - on water and land."

— Walt Whitman

Radical freedom demands self-authority. This means you look to no one for permission to be exactly who you feel yourself to be. No one gets to put their hooks into you and lead you this way or that way. With self-authority requires self-responsibility. Needless to say, this paradigm does not sit well with a society bent on enforcing rules and supporting institutions that demand obedience. This step is an opportunity to grab your authority and take it back. Why give your power away? Who does that serve? It certainly does not serve you. Yet many of us have been raised in a society with several fundamental authority figures. Grab your authority and give it back to yourself. It is not easy, as there are a plethora of people and entities demanding your feasance.

For the first four years of grade school, I attended Mass six days a week. My only day off from going to Mass was Saturday. I don't really know what the purpose of sending 6 year old children to a large building to listen to a priest speak Latin, but back in the 60s, it was the thing to do.

I fondly remember kneeling in the pews, letting my tongue touch the wood of the pew in front of me. It had a very unusual and appealing taste to me, so I would taste it often. I remember being bored most of the time, since I didn't really understand what was happening up there in the front. Things did improve slightly once I received my first holy communion and I was able to participate in that sacrament during my second grade. The best part of going to church on school days was the end. I remember experiencing pure exuberance when I could walk out the doors of the church, into the sunshine, and onto the school playground. I loved to play. That was all that really mattered to me, playing. Going to church, going to school, doing chores, those were all things that needed to be done so that I would have time to play.

I was raised with a few significant authority figures. First were my parents. Second was the church, which was an amalgam of individuals: teachers, priests, and nuns. Third was God portrayed as a being in heaven that held the keys to my salvation. It wasn't until I left my childhood home to attend Cal Berkeley that I could get some distance and look somewhat objectively at all the things I was taught. The more I looked, the more free I felt, as I was able to release these authority figures, and come to realize I could look to myself and my experiences for answers.

Lately, a group of people that spend time doing similar activities is now referred to as a tribe. For example, I have a blog to which many people subscribe. I refer to this group of people as a tribe, as my tribe. I also spend many weekends attending transformational events with men and women, and also refer to the group as a tribe. Some tribes do not claim authority, while others do. I will only be a member of a tribe that does not. Ultimately, I am a tribe of one. In the end, when you look at life with the clearest of vision, there are no others.

A few years back, I attended a weekend event. During the weekend, I met a young man in his twenties. He spoke of how his friends, and various girls with which he had approached to go out on a date, treated him with disdain. In a beautiful expression of rage, he screamed out,

"Fuck 'em all!" I do love to see those moments of clarity, rare as they are. Later in the event, I had a chance to acknowledge this young man. I said, "I honor your willingness to walk your own path. Like you, I am a tribe of one."

Much of life is about un-learning. In my early twenties, I soon realized I was absolutely not a part of the Catholic tribe. There were too many rules that simply didn't make any sense when contrasted to my experience of life. However, when I declared my resignation from the tribe, I was met with a strong voice from my family, a voice of disapproval. I have come to learn that when one leaves the tribe, the remaining tribe members display a wide range of emotions: anger, sadness, fear, and confusion. Dealing with this disapproval, and understanding its deep, underlying and dark roots, is a seminal piece of the life long process of waking up. It forces one inward.

Next, again in my twenties, I determined that being married simply was something I could no longer do. I had been married for 7 years, had two children, and was completely miserable. Looking back now, I can see that the misery was my own, and that blaming it on my wife was childish. But at the time, my reality was such that I believed changing my external world would impact my internal world, and moving on was the decision I made.

Well, here again, getting a divorce brings up a titanic deluge of disapproval, not only from close family members, but from anyone who is married. Marriage is a tribe. I was the first in my family to get a divorce. My parents are still married, as are my two brothers. It is not too strong to say that my divorce created such a rift in my family that my membership was temporarily revoked. I was no longer a part of the tribe of my immediate family. I was not invited to Thanksgiving, nor was I spoken to. It was some months later that my father approached me and rekindled communication. Here again, I learned how the other tribe members respond when one of their own either breaks the rules or leaves.

There is yet another tribe to which I have been a part, which attracts those who have rejected various other tribes such as religion, marriage, government and family. It is deceptive, for when you join this tribe it feels like you really belong. Author Stuart Wilde coined the phrase "fringe dwellers." I hang out with various groups that fall into this classification. In Sebastopol, California, where I live, you see fringe dwellers everywhere. Many tribe members even wear a sort of uniform to let everyone know they have exited the mainstream, and live a declared life of freedom from all of society's trappings. Hemp clothing is a big clue that you are among a band of fringe dwellers. Talking about crystals, moon phases, and the next music festival are also strong clues. However, here again, as I have often done, when I speak my truth with contrary beliefs, I get a strong dose of disapproval from tribe members.

All of this raises the question, why is there a need to be a part of a tribe? From where does the demanding desire to be secure in a group or community come? I would say it comes from a lack of trust and a feeling of disconnection. This desire to be a part of a group is a reaction to a feeling of being separate. It is a way to fill a hole. It serves to provide comfort to those in pain. Rather than go inward to find the peace we all want, we look to the support of a group to provide that connection. Instead of connecting with our god, or higher power, or whatever you would call it, we connect with like-minded beings and find solace in the sameness.

God, or the belief in a god, is the biggest authority figure in existence. Virtually all cultures on this planet have a belief is a supreme deity. Here in America, for the most part, we just refer to this being as God. Most are raised to believe in God. Political and religious institutions ram this belief down our throats from the day we are born. "God bless America." It is even on our money: "In God We Trust." The belief goes like this: There is a supreme being, and his (or her, if you are a member of the Goddess tribe) job is to listen to your prayers, and take care of you. The more you live your life a certain way, and follow the rules, the better your life will be. Hence the God tribe is born. When all is lost and you are forlorn, you can always join up with God, and feel the safety and security for which many long. I have heard expressions like, "I was saved!" or, "I was born again!" to express the jubilation of joining the God tribe.

Being a member of the God tribe requires faith, for there is no proof of the existence of God. At this point in my life, I prefer to do without faith. My mind simply won't allow me to believe in anything. If I experience something and know it to be true, then I have something to say. If anyone is going to tell me that I must believe, or trust, or have faith, then I will suggest they aren't looking deep enough. I have looked deep. I have a powerful innate drive to dig as deep as necessary into my seedy murky dark side to get to some truth. Superstitions don't interest me. God, as taught to me, is a superstition. However, it is undeniable that there is a force, a power, an intelligence that oversees our existence. This I have experienced over and over again.

There can be a tremendous amount of pain that accompanies the separation from a tribe. A dear friend of mine is now going through a separation from her immediate family. As I see it, her energy has recently risen, and those who can't handle the energy, are rejecting her. Not only is it a lesson in letting go, but also in honoring the powerful direction of a life. Some things can't be undone. You can't un-pop a balloon. And why would you want to? Our powerlessness is complete and undeniable. We all have a choice. We can row the boat in the direction of the current, or struggle and suffer and row against the current, all because we think we know what is best, or what is right.

There are not many people I know that are independent thinkers. It is just too damned hard! Everyone thinks they think for themselves. That is obvious. But really, truly, most do not. We are raised from cradle to grave to honor authority figures. We give so much of our power away to these thoughts, these people, these institutions, and we do it with a smile on our face, for we feel we are choosing these actions of our own free will. In truth, we are sheep being led through life. Challenging any belief system is very difficult to do. It is like going through a divorce. Thinking for yourself, and not relying on the belief system of any particular group is scary stuff.

If you are going to pursue a life of radical freedom, you will have to go your own way. You just can't be a part of the tribe, and be radically free. To be radically free means you have developed your own philosophy of life. It is yours and yours alone. Your philosophy is not developed from shared beliefs, dogma, or childhood influences. Every thought you have ever believed myst be questioned, and challenged, and whittled down to its core or essence. Your philosophy is simple, but it was not simple to get to.

Going your own way does not mean being anti-social or living in isolation. It means you have done the heavy lifting, which must be done alone, and in doing that work, you have seen for yourself what is and what is not true. It is a solo journey. There are times in which a group may support you in your development. There is an undeniable power in group dynamics. Major leaps in consciousness can be made in a group environment. But those leaps must then be integrated and this is the tough individual work.

There is a movie called *Heat* staring Robert DeNiro. In it, DeNiro plays a bright and ruthless criminal. He explains to his love interest that to remain free, one must be able to walk away from everything and everybody in one's life within 30 seconds time. At the end of the movie, he is unable to walk away and is then captured and dies at the hands of the Al Pacino character. This is a wonderful example of the nature of radical freedom. Can you be so present, and so clear, that possessions and people in your life are temporary, that you would be able to walk away within 30 seconds? *Heat* is a movie, and you would never have to leave everything and everybody in your life within 30 seconds, but could you? It is a stinging litmus test for radical freedom.

"In what concerns you much, do not think that you have companions: know that you are alone in the world."

—Henry David Thoreau

This is the brutal truth. There is no other. You are alone in the world. Everything is a reflection of you. Metaphysically speaking, we are all made up of the same thing, energy. Duality is the illusion. When people experience Samadhi, they experience everything as one. The illusion is shattered. Again, the hard work after an experience such as this is integrating it into your life while living in a world that functions with duality as reality. Picture a salmon swimming upstream against the current. This is what going your own way looks and feels like, at least for a while.

There is a way, which is the same way for all who live in radical freedom, which was arrived at by each person going his or her own way. All paths lead to the same conclusion. Yes, one man's path is not your path, and vice versa. You can't cross the river by using a boat. The way across the river requires a different level of consciousness. You can't get there from here. This is where grace must come to you and support you and elevate you so that you can make the final crusade.

This step is an invitation to break away from the pack and become your own ultimate authority. Stop being a sheep, one of the herd, doing all the herd things. You know you have a path. You know you want to discover what is truly going on in this lifetime. You desire to discover truth and freedom. The only thing that will stop you is fear of the unknown. You don't know how hard it will be. You don't know what it will feel like to be different than the other members of your various tribes. The only way you will know is to go your own way.

"So remember one basic law: life is insecurity. And if you are ready to live in insecurity, only then will you be alive. Insecurity is freedom. If you are ready to be insecure, constantly insecure, you will be free. And freedom is the door to the divine."

—Osho

Assignment:

I invite you to take some time and do some journaling. During your journaling, the questions to ask yourself are: Where do I give my power away? To whom (person or institution) do I give authority over any aspect of my life? What beliefs do I have as a result of these authority figures? What would be different if I did not have these beliefs?

Step 6

Action, Ready, Set

Go jump off a cliff. Don't go near the cliff and contemplate jumping off. Don't read a book about jumping off. Don't study the art and science of jumping off. Don't join a support group for jumping off. Don't write poems about jumping off. Don't kiss the ass of someone else who jumped off. Just jump.

—Jed McKenna

You will not be able to create anything of lasting importance without taking action. I often hear the phrase "massive action" to emphasize the necessity of taking action to get something accomplished. Paralysis by analysis is so prevalent that we have a clever rhyming name for it. You have to get in the habit of doing things, taking actions that will move you in the direction of your vision. Otherwise, nothing is going to get accomplished. You can create a vision board, cut photos out of magazines, include your favorite role models, but without action, you just created a daily reminder of what you are not going to achieve!

Let me share with you the Law of Marsha. Marsha is a woman I have worked with over the past 10 years organizing 3-day weekend workshops. During our first event together, Marsha told me, in regards to enrolling people into the workshop, to consistently put out the energy for people to hear about the event, and consistently put out the energy to follow up. The Law of Marsha states that all of that energy will come back in one way or another. The beauty of the law is that I can rest in the knowledge that my focus need only be on putting out the energy, and the universe will respond back in kind.

As I have learned, the results won't always appear as I might expect. For example, I may send out a flurry of emails, yet not get any direct response. However, a friend who I have not spoken to in years will call me and ask about the next workshop and sign up. There is not necessarily a direct one to one correlation, but the law has always demonstrated itself to be true. The way the law is expressed by Marsha is this: "Keep putting it out, keep putting it out, and it will always come back."

Another pertinent question before taking action is this: What action shall I take? The Pareto principle, also known as the 80/20 rule, states that 80% of the results come from 20% of the causes. Or another way to put it is 20% of your thoughts and actions produce 80% of your results. So, the question we all need to be looking at is what are the key actions that produce the greatest result? Let's take writing a book as an example. The actual act of writing is the most important action. I can think about writing, which is not writing. I can sit at my keyboard and daydream, and that is not writing. No, actually typing these words into my MacBook Pro is the action. If I can do that for a minimum of 2 hours a day, I will write a book in about 6 months. All the other actions won't get the book written. Focus on the 20% of the actions that produce 80% of the results.

It is also important to perform your actions with excellence. Meet Boyd. Boyd is the proprietor of the ZZ House in Chiang Mai, Thailand. Boyd is 40 years old, a true professional, and as nice as a guy can be. He doesn't see his patrons as dollar signs, but rather as human beings who want to have a great time while visiting his hotel and beautiful Thai city. The second night I was there in Chiang Mai, Boyd took all his patrons to a Buddhist Lantern Festival. He drove us one hour out of town to the venue, pointed us in the right direction, met us afterwards for the drive back, and insured that we had the time of our lives. That night was as glorious as an experience as I have had. Most any other hotels may have told me about the event, but how would I know how to get there, where to park, what to bring, etc. I am, after all, an American who is visiting Thailand. With Boyd going well above and beyond the call of duty, I had an evening I will never forget.

Doing anything with excellence has its own rewards. The pride of creating a product or service that powerfully rings of excellence is profound. Seeing others experience excellence is equally empowering. Knowing that you did the best you could, to create something that potently and positively impacts others, allows you to sleep better at night. I did my best. That is all I can do. I did not take any shortcuts. I did not cheat anyone. I did not make a few extra bucks by omitting this or that. No, I went for it 100% and let the chips fall where they may.

When I think about taking a short cut, or doing it the easy way, or settling for good enough rather than great, I will remember my Thai friend Boyd and his approach to life and work. Always give them more than they expect. And expect nothing in return. That sounds like a fantastic recipe for life. It is simple and profound and surprisingly uncommon.

The other thing about action is it can be somewhat, if not very, monotonous. Writing, for example, can at times be a chore. Talking to 40 clients in a row can be, at times, less than stimulating. Once you find something you are good at, you will, no doubt, do it over and over again. Let me tell you the rest of the story about the woman in the cowboy hat to really make this important point.

I found the woman in the cowboy hat who serves stewed pork leg at her stand just outside of the Old City at the north wall in Chiang Mai, Thailand. It was a phenomenal meal. It reminded me of my mom's beef pot roast, but with pork and a slightly thinner, although unbelievably tasty, sauce. Some people are pork people and others are beef people. I am a pork guy. It is like you are either an Elvis or Beatles person. Sorry Elvis.

I had read that the woman in the cowboy hat started her shift at 5 PM, so I arrived a little bit early thinking her stand might quickly get crowded on a Saturday night. I could tell I had found her stand when I saw her picture emblazoned street side. There were 3 guys getting things set up, putting the pork on the stand, cooking rice, cleaning tables, etc. I walked around looking for something to drink. Then I saw her walking toward her stand. I said "It's you. I saw you 6 months ago on American TV and now I am here." She nodded, smiled, pointed to her stand, and continued walking. I realized I might have been a bit too exuberant for her as she started her shift. And clearly she has heard this more than a few times.

After I got my drink, I returned to her stand, and saw I could sit at a table, and someone would take my order and bring me the stewed pork goodness. As I sat there, in the dining area behind the stand, I watched her work. Then it dawned on me. While this is all very exciting for me, a dream realized, a new taste treat experienced, everyday for the past 6 months since I saw her on TV, our woman in the cowboy hat has been standing there at her stand, moving a stewed pork leg to her chopping block, skillfully extracting the meat from the bone, chopping the pork into bite size bits, and serving it up on a plate of rice. All the while, she is dressed in fine clothes, wears a cowboy hat, and never seems to get a drop of pork stew on her.

I know there is a myth that implies that every moment may be filled with bliss. Follow your passion, and do what you love, and everyday will be filled with rainbows and unicorns. Anyone who has gone down this road will tell you this bliss myth is utter crap. Our woman in the cowboy hat looks to have it all. She makes good money here in Thailand. She is famous. I watched 5 different people within 30 minutes walk up to her and take pictures. She owns her own business. She has been on television. And she is beautiful. All of this supports the myth.

Still, every day for 6 or more hours, she stands in one little spot, and chops the pork. There must be times where she says to herself, "If I have to chop one more pork leg, I think I am going to scream!" or "If another American man comes up to me to tell me his story, I am going to throw my cleaver at him!" But she doesn't. Every day she chops. Everyday she deals with the pictures and notoriety. Everyday she puts out an amazing product for the world to enjoy. As I sat there observing her while she prepared my dish, my appreciation for her grew.

I was reminded in that moment that those of us who want to get something done in the world, we work. We work when it is new and exciting, and we work when it feels a bit like drudgery. It doesn't matter how we feel. We are clear that this is what we are to do to get the results we want, and so we do it. It is the consistency that demonstrates maturity. We don't work sometimes, or when we feel like it. We work. We produce. We have pride in the quality of our work. We deliver.

It is the consistency that impresses me. The woman in the cowboy hat stands and chops. Day in and day out, she chops. She wears a big ol' cowboy hat no matter how hot and humid it is in Chiang Mai. She serves the best tasting pork stew I have ever tasted. Day in and day out, she stands for 6 hours serving up dish after dish. Every day she chops. Everyday, she is my hero.

I invite you to keep thinking about your most actiony action. What is the thing you need to do to get where you want to get? As an Internet marketing coach, the most important action is talking to my clients on the phone. The more I do that, the more success I will have. As a writer, the action is writing. The more writing I do, the better a writer I will be. As a father, the action is speaking with my children, as opposed to, for example, watching television with them.

Let's end this step with a short prayer.

It's time to stop playing small. That little voice in my head is not me and so I refuse to listen to its pernicious ego whisperings. I will give all I have to give. I will be generous with my life's story, no matter how vulnerable and exposed I feel. It is my privilege.

I will work day by day to develop the habits and obtain the knowledge to support me on my quest. It is a hero's quest we are all on. The quest is for the fullest expression of who I am. This is where my gifts are to be found. This is the stuff of which an amazing life, my life, is born, nurtured and brought to an explosion of love and bliss and ultimate contentment.

I will play big starting now. I choose to live as a fully realized adult. I will flow with the universe and allow myself to be fully used by every atom of creation. I surrender. I Let Go. I gladly give. I am at the edge and leaping off into the great unknown. The space outside of my comfort zone will be my home.

Today truly is the first day of my life. I embrace the magnificence that lives within me, that is me and that is you, too.

This is my law of existence. So may it be.

Assignment:

Your assignment is threefold. What is it that you most want to accomplish within the next 30 days? Pick just one thing. Next, what is the most important action you can take to achieve your goal? And finally, every day, take that action. You will be simply amazed at what you can achieve. Discover your most actiony actions and then act on them.

Step 7

Slow Down

*"Do you have the patience to wait
till your mud settles and the water is clear?
Can you remain unmoving
till the right action arises by itself?"*

—Tao Te Ching. Chapter 15

Life for most of us moves pretty darned fast. I don't know when the word multitasking came into existence, but everyone is doing it! In order to survive in today's world, you and I have to get a whole bunch of things done. Not just today, but every day! I wake up at 3:30 AM just so I can have a little bit of me time. A typical day includes a trip to the health club, breakfast, lunch and dinner, a full 8 hour work day, handling logistics such as laundry, bills, gas for the car, repairs, doctor, dentist, children, errands, attentive time for a relationship, feed the dog or cat, and on and on. How do we do it? More importantly, why do we do it?

My parents told me I was born with a certain drive to do things well. Does this sound familiar? Go to school. Get good grades. Go to college. Graduate with a good job. Get married. Have children. Work hard. Retire. Enjoy the grandchildren. Now none of this sounds bad. In fact, it sounds pretty good. And so, I have lived a good chunk of my life chasing these things, almost in blind obedience to a false idol called Success. In order to achieve these things, we have to work very hard, chasing after our particular vision of success, forsaking our inner life to a great extent.

For many, this is life. Go! Go! Go! I loved it. The tribe loves it. Adrenaline kicks in and life is one event after another. It may be exhausting. It may be spiritually barren. It may be unhealthy. It may seem pointless and meaningless. But if you buy into the vision, it works. That is until one starts to question the vision. Who's vision? Why the vision? Ignorance is bliss! This book will seem like utter silliness to those who are in the throes of society's expectations. Still there are a few of us ready to jump off the merry-go-round, ask a few very serious questions, and take a long and deep look within.

"The quieter you become, the more you can hear."

—Ram Dass

Given that we have spent most of our lifetime doing things, we have developed a habit of ongoing activity. We do not like to spend much time without doing things. We have a hard time being still. We get itchy with nothing to do. It is particularly noticeable now that we all have smartphones. The smartphone is quickly replacing conversation as our modus operandi. Even when we have free time, we fill up that free time with more, and often mindless, activities. I admit I have been a master of distractions. I consumed distractions every chance I could. I have loved distractions since I can remember.

Examples of distractions are going to a movie, dating, drinking, smoking, having sex, masturbating, spending money, exercising, listening to music, eating, or reading the latest spy novel. And television (how could I forget the 30 bleeps per second of television) is perhaps the strongest distraction, foisted upon us and gratefully consumed in large quantities to distract us from the real business of living. These things are all ways in which we can, essentially, medicate ourselves against feeling what it is to just be. How can we learn anything about ourselves when our heads are in the clouds?

Of course, these distractions are also wonderful components of a life fully lived. I enjoy movies, books, a loving relationship, and eating all foods as much as anyone. It is when these activities are used not to enjoy life, but to hide from life, that something is missing. The key is the intention of the activity. We all know when we are using an activity as a distraction, as a way to run and hide from our fear of simply being alone with ourselves. In the end, it comes down to finding a balance, a natural symbiosis in which our alone time is cherished, and our time in action is untethered and proactive rather than reactive. It is a matter of balance and self-discipline. I believe we can have it all.

Distractions numb us, cloud our minds, and sap us of vital energy we could be using on more productive and life enriching activities. Distractions are like children's toys. They don't serve adults and they become painful when you start to see them for what they are, more of a burden to carry along with you than anything else. At some point, we may choose to put them down. We seem to realize at some point in our life that we don't have to feel special, elevated, or happy all the time. When that special moment of malaise starts to sink in, you won't need to grab another piece of pie or check your emails. Rather, you sit with it, question it, and continue to discover just what makes you tick. It is in that knowing that true peace and serenity live.

Life used to feel to me like a high-speed rail train. The train is moving very fast. I can, at times, look out the window and see my life going by. Still, the train is moving so fast, I can only focus on a few things at a time because the scenery keeps changing as we rocket down the rails. The invitation here is to slow down the train, and start to get a sense of a life moving at a slower pace. Life will still move at the same speed, but your experience of it will slow down. If you can think of your experience of life as one of looking through a particular lens, which filters everything you see or experience, then we are talking about making a subtle shift in the lens so things get much clearer and understandable and real.

How do we slow down our experience of the train? Where do we get the patience to allow the mud to settle and have the water become clear? Even though the ideas of peace and serenity are starting to whisper in our ear and blow a cool breeze into our heart, it is difficult to get the process of slowing down underway. It is so easy to find a distraction. The television is always there, as is the food in the kitchen, and the relationship that feels oh so good. It takes a level of adult maturity to set aside some time for ME. It takes courage to put down all the distractions, and learn to become still. It takes patience to begin a discipline of reclaiming your birthright to experience a deep level of serenity. And finally, it takes a powerful vision to empower you to take the first step to jump off the high-speed train of life in search of something that is not necessarily glamorous, yet is so essential to our well-being.

"The power of quiet is great. It generates the same feelings in everything one encounters. It vibrates with the cosmic rhythm of oneness. It is everywhere, available to anyone at any time. It is us, the force within that makes us stable, trusting, and loving. It is contemplation contemplating us. Peace is letting go – returning to the silence that cannot enter the realm of words, because it is too pure to be contained in words. This why the tree, the stone, the river, and the mountain are quiet."

—Malidoma Patrice Some

When we slow down and take a deep breath, we can feel the touch of God (universal energy, nature, flow, force…) in everything. There is no question that this force is everywhere. Everything is comprised of this energy. It does take some effort to train oneself to perceive reality just as it is. When we add all kinds of extra filters and beliefs and false notions to our life experience, God gets squeezed out. I look outside my window and see a red tail hawk flying in a circle overhead, and I melt. I walk down the street and see the sparkle in the eyes of the people that meet my gaze. I enjoy a cup of coffee in the morning, which brings up fond memories of my childhood. God is everywhere if we look for her. The real question is how we feel God in everything so we don't feel a lack. If we don't feel a separation from God, then our desire for the sacred does not drive us to undertake extreme activities that are not healthy or productive. How do we manage ourselves so our drive for the divine is not creating chaos in our lives? How can we insert balance into our lives so we can have it all, live lives in which we feel content, and not feel we have to find something, anything to fill a hole inside of ourselves? Let's move forward to look for some answers.

Assignment:

Today, take 20 minutes during your day to sit down, preferably in nature, and do nothing but observe life as it is happening right in front of you. Sit, do nothing, and observe.

Step 8

Courage

"Putting things off is the biggest waste of life: it snatches away each day as it comes, and denies us the present by promising the future. The greatest obstacle to living is expectancy, which hangs upon tomorrow, and loses today. You are arranging what lies in Fortune's control, and abandoning what lies in yours. What are you looking at? To what goal are you straining? The whole future lies in uncertainty: live immediately."

—Seneca

We can learn from the cowardly lion. The pursuit of the radical freedom takes a massive amount of courage, the courage to take action now. This is particularly true in the beginning of the journey. Once you start walking the path, energy takes over and you don't have much choice but to hold on and allow the rapids of life to take you on your merry way.

It takes courage to look at your essence, for you, at your core, are an amalgam of light and dark. It takes courage to begin the process of knowing yourself. It is easy to look and see all the good stuff. The trick is to look at the dark stuff, come to terms with it, appreciate it, rather than pretend it does not exist, and integrate it into your being. I have discovered that I am competitive. I relish the thought of winning and another losing. I have rage and anger and impatience that live within me. I have the capacity to kill. These are just some of the components of my dark side. It is my journey to discover these aspects of myself and come to a place of acceptance. In order to truly experience your authentic self, this has to happen. Since our self-knowledge and self-acceptance is incomplete, we look outside of ourselves for more. And so we have a culture that celebrates celebrities, possessions, and living vicariously through television, films and books. We hear the expression, "You complete me." If only more looked within, wherein lie all the answers.

So where do you start? The elixir is in the poison. You courageously dive into the hurt. I have never met a human being that did not have some feelings of self-loathing. Often it is self-loathing, like the pain from a persistent pebble in our shoe, which awakens us to action. It's the discomfort that creates the yearning for something greater. It's only in the acquisition of self-knowledge that we begin to appreciate the brilliance of our human condition. It's this appreciation for the universal condition of all beings that begins to look like self-love. But it is not self-love. It is love.

In my life, I displayed the courage to ask a powerful mystic to be my teacher. I had no idea what I had asked for, or how intense and brutal the lessons would be. My time with this fellow culminated one day in the garden out behind an English cottage in the London suburbs. I was 40 years old at the time, and I would have to say I was a meek young man. I rejected my masculinity. I preferred spending time with women. I was a sensitive new age guy (aka SNAG) who was getting along all right in the world. Honestly, I didn't think I was missing anything. My life was satisfactory. Others hoped to emulate the relationship I had with my wife.

Then one day, everything changed. I got really angry. I got so angry that I knew I could kill. And in that moment, I began to scratch the surface of a part of me that was dormant. I felt like a lion that had just learned how to roar. And it felt good.

In my case, it took an older man, my teacher, confronting me on the way I was living my life to turn the key, to open the lock to my full masculinity. He was physical with me, and brutally honest in a way that I could not defend (more on this later in the book). And it pissed me off. From that experience, a primal yearning began to emerge. I wanted to kill. I wanted to kill him. I wanted to defend. And beyond all that, I wanted to make a contribution to the world. Rather than sucking off the fat of the land as I had been doing for so long, I was committed to discovering all aspects of myself and sharing my learning with others. None of this occurs without the courage to ask for guidance. I knew I was playing with fire, and I certainly did burn. Painful as it was, a bigger part of me did not care about collateral damage. My desire for self-knowledge was too great.

When people look into my eyes, they trust me, for in these eyes they experience a man who had the courage to undertake the process of self-immolation. Going into your dark and nasty ugliness is tough work. Getting to know your own dark demons is essential if you are to move forward on the path of evolving consciousness. Pretending to be nice, and honest, and sincere all looks fake until you have done the real work of self-discovery. Only in being courageous and going toward the darkness, and feeling the pain of your humanity can you discover the brightest of your lights.

Assignment:

What is it you need to do today, but are afraid to do? What action can you take that would require courage? What makes you uncomfortable, yet you know you must do it to move forward in your life. Go and do it.

Step 9

Meditation

"None of us will ever accomplish anything excellent or commanding except when he listens to this whisper which is heard by him alone."

— Ralph Waldo Emerson

Stillness. Quiet of heart. A facile mind. Easy. Time slows. Nature's rhythm. Everything has the same message. It is not in words. It is a feeling, an all-pervading tidal wave of sheer presence. Do you feel it? The enormity of it is awesome, as in full of, drop to your knees, awe and wonder. It flows from everything and through everything. It is the current of life. It is the breath of existence. It is our sustenance. It is devastating in its power and simplicity. It is with us at all times, and it is only our manipulations that keep us from experiencing it. It has been called love, and bliss, and light, and God, and in the end, no words can describe that which is always present. It can't be found, for it was never lost. When you get it, you will ache. The only reason you or I feel lonely is because we feel a lack, and we think another will eliminate our sense of lack. Meditation will teach you that you lack nothing, and your time by yourself is your most precious and cherished time. Loneliness be gone.

Meditation is a profound way to raise one's energy. In the process of slowing things down by taking in some quiet time, your emotions, feelings, upsets, and thoughts all become muted, allowing for more pure energy to exist. The paradigm is this: You are nothing but pure energy. Being full of pure energy is our natural state. Throughout our lifetime, we have established some bad habits, some unhealthy ways of experiencing our world. We begin to have beliefs about a wide range of topics that simply are not true. This in turn causes disharmony and disease. As we create more disharmony and disease, our energy gets slower and slower, flatter and flatter.

The value of meditation has been well documented. Purely physical responses to meditation include lower blood pressure, better circulation, more calmness, less stress, and enhanced memory. Unfortunately, many people hear the word meditation, and think of monks in robes, and hours and hours of work, when this is simply not the case. It is true that your ego won't like meditation at first. It is like training a dog. Your ego will object to your meditation time. This will only last a few minutes. You have to let your mind spin out for a while, protest, confuse, and attempt all sorts of mayhem to convince you meditation is not a good idea. Thank it for sharing.

Meditation is a seminal key to your liberation and transcendence. You will begin to understand the dynamics of your own mind. You will begin to understand and make distinctions about your own consciousness. You will be able to tap into your higher power and receive guidance and bits of information to guide you on your path. And you will flat out feel better. It is wonderful to begin to learn more about your self and open and access inner worlds.

Meditation is a tangible and easy tool to implement the discipline to tame and ultimately transcend the ego. You will get away from all the noise, the TV, the competition, the rat race. It is important to be clear on your intention. See yourself where your want to be. Have a vision. Stay with it. It will be tough at times, for you won't always be able to see progress, nor understand how impactful is your meditation practice. Without a doubt, meditation is one of the most potent ways to learn who you really are, and more importantly, unlearn who you think you are.

One goal of a meditation practice is to transcend this conditional experience and realize you are a spiritual being. You truly are a spirit inside a body that you are just renting for a time. The silence, the stillness, the abundance of nothingness, this is where the power is. Meditation can get you to the place where everything is ok just the way it is. Through this process, you will begin to dissolve the self loathing that so many live with, and achieve complete self acceptance.

Meditation is a powerful tool we can all use to slow down our experience of life on the fast moving train. Meditation is something you can do anywhere at any time in your life. You can meditate with your eyes open, or with your eyes closed. You can do it standing up, or sitting down. The only requirements for meditation are that you have an intention to meditate and that you do it alone.

Meditation is simply the act of being quiet with yourself. In the act of being quiet, you will become intimate with the workings of your mind, and begin to understand how it is your mind, and your relationship with your self, play a supreme role in how you experience your life. In general, the results of meditation are clarity, a greater sense of well-being, a feeling of unity, and a shift towards a more peaceful existence.

"You should sit in meditation 20 minutes every day, unless you're too busy, then you should sit for an hour."

— Old Zen Adage

How often you choose to meditate, and how you meditate, are up to you. I recommend a minimum of 20 minutes per day. That is enough to allow anyone to begin to get a taste of what is possible through this ancient activity. There are all types of ways to meditate. I have found the simplest approach is to sit comfortably in silence. In the silence, I simply listen to my mind. At first, it is anything but silent. My mind has a bunch to say.

"Hmmm, so here I am."

Then I will hear myself talking about work, errands to run, or just about anything that has happened or will be happening in the future.

"Breathe, Jay. Just focus on your breath."

"In... Out... In... Out..."

Then I will hear some more chatter about work, etc., though not as much...

"Breathe, Jay. Just focus on your breath."

"In... Out... In... Out..."

At some point, I get still. My mind gets tired of speaking. My ego takes a break. My predominant thought is on my breath going in and out. And then even that thought is silenced. I have been meditating for over 20 years, so my ability to still my mind happens faster than it would for a person trying mediation for the first time. When starting out, your goal is simply to sit for 20 minutes in silence. Don't expect your mind to stop much, and do expect your mind to react with a whole bunch of words and thoughts and feelings. The lesson is to surrender to it all, be still, focus on your breath, and observe the chatter.

Say yes. Don't ask for a contract. Don't ask for an explanation to be worked out. It is an intuitive thing—a call. And you feel this call also. A call into silence. Into timelessness, into space, into wisdom, into love, into the all encompassing one. Say yes to this thing. Unreservedly. Because your mind will do everything to stop you from this.

—Mooji

But after a time, your mind does get tired of itself, and the meditation becomes far more silent. Silence is not the goal of meditation. There is no goal. All there is to do is observe. At some point during meditation, it becomes clear there is a speaker and a listener. When I say to myself, "Breathe, Jay. Just focus on your breath," who am I speaking to? Who is speaking? Who is listening? You don't have to meditate to observe this dichotomy. All day we are "talking to ourselves." Who is *we*?

Who is *ourselves*? In being a human being, we experience a duality, an experience of a speaker, and an experience of a listener.

Right now you can close your eyes, and meditate. I can be waiting in line, and while other people are angry and elevating their blood pressure, I can close me eyes, or not, and be still and quiet. Every moment is an opportunity for silence, for a dive into the divine, or a message from your inner wisdom. This is the real deal. If you are serious about radical freedom, meditation is a powerful key to unlock the door.

Assignment:

The assignment is to meditate for a minimum of 20 minutes. These are some simple, easy to follow instructions for setting up a meditation session:

1. Set a time. Take a stand.

2. Do it at any time of the day.

3. Do it for a minimum of 20 to 30 minutes.

4. Set a challenge for yourself, say 30 days.

5. Sit down.

6. Light a candle and place it in front of you.

7. Breathe in and out. Full breath.

8. Tense a muscle and then relax it. Do this through your body from your feet to your head.

9. Just notice the thoughts.

10. When thoughts seem loud, put the focus on your breath, in and out.

11. Let the thoughts pass. They are not you. Stay with it. Don't stop.

Step 10

Responding vs. Reacting

*"If she's amazing, she won't be easy. If she's easy, she won't be amazing.
If she's worth it, you won't give up. If you give up, you're not worthy. ... Truth
is, everybody is going to hurt you; you just gotta find the ones
worth suffering for."*

— Bob Marley

Mind The Gap. When I traveled to Paris, I used the French subway system, called the Metro, to get around. I saw a sign up seemingly everywhere: Mind The Gap. This always made me laugh because, to me, this phrase was not referring to the gap between the station floor and the subway train, but instead had referred to the space in time between experiencing something, and then taking an appropriate action in response.

Someone who does not mind the gap, rather than responding to a situation, will react, often to his or her own peril. Let's look at a simple and prevalent situation in our society, domestic violence. A woman says something to her man that upsets the man. The man reacts and slaps her across the face. This is pure reaction. She spoke. Anger is triggered. He, without thinking about the woman or the consequences, strikes the woman. What if he had the awareness to handle the situation differently? Woman speaks. Anger is triggered. Man recognizes that anger is triggered. Man comprehends that in relationships, suffering is bound to occur. Man understand the anger is his own, his responsibility, and the woman is serving as a catalyst, and man walks away to take a walk and assess why her words triggered anger.

Life is full of triggers. A key to our sanity seems to be in understanding what the dynamics are of a reaction. In our earlier example, the woman's words are a trigger. What she triggered was an earlier upset, something very similar in nature, which hurt the man such that he still feels incredible pain when he is reminded of the hurt. The key here is that the man is not reacting to the woman's words, but to the memories and feelings they bring up. I have heard this referred to as a stack attack, meaning we have a stack of memories, painful, hurtful memories, and when they are yanked up into our consciousness, we feel under attack and want to lash out in reaction. If you don't understand the mechanism, it looks like the man is reacting to the woman's words. That is not the case. It is what those words stir up from the past that is the real source of anger.

The only way I have seen to drive this point home is for someone to recall the last time they felt angry, and then invite them to go back in time to an earlier incident that produced the same feelings. Then go back even further until you get to the first incident. This seems to alleviate the feelings, as one begins to see how the specific behavior worked back then (usually as a way to protect), but now as a more mature and self-aware adult, that behavior does not work. I shared earlier about my experience in sixth grade. Much of my needy and clinging behavior resulted from the initial incident. Once I saw this clearly, I was free to respond to situations, rather than react with feelings of fear and abandonment. Then the choice became to respond to the present moment rather than to a past experience. This choice leads to either happiness or unhappiness.

"Unhappiness is caused by comparison. You feel unhappy only when you unconsciously compare your present state with another state, perhaps when you were younger or healthier, or perhaps when you had a certain companion or possessed certain public honors. Where there is no comparison, unhappiness is impossible. Happiness exists when the mind does not move away from itself, when it remains in the present time zone, when it declines to contrast itself with another time or another condition."

—Vernon Howard

The other shift that must occur is the one to full ownership of our own feelings, emotions, reactions and responses. Often during our men's group meetings, a man will rail against his wife, his boss, his upbringing or his victimization, all of which usually leads to anger. The reminder is "the anger is your own!" We have to stop putting any blame on outside influences. Your Dad may have been a real bastard, but it is you that is getting angry. Own it. Beginning to understand these dynamics will allow you to put some distance between a trigger and a response. It is the first step toward liberation from pure, out of control, reaction.

Assignment:

Mind the gap. To start out, when you feel the urge to yell or scream or hit, make an agreement to take 10 deep breaths, and think about the appropriate response. Usually it is to walk away, get in nature, write down your feelings, and see if you can take the feelings back to their origin. There in lies the elixir.

Step 11

Inside Out

"People always assume that freedom consists in getting something desirable from the exterior world, when in fact it consists exclusively of getting rid of something undesirable in the interior world."

— Vernon Howard

In order to achieve what you want, you must do the inner work. Nothing will manifest on the outside until transformation occurs on the inside. For many, this process occurs as a result of a powerful life event, be it a loss of a job, a death of a loved one, an illness, or any of the many ways we are challenged throughout our life. The result of this is that we are forced to look within, not without, to find some answers, not only about our situation, but more so about ourselves.

We live in an Outside In society. Look at our world as it is today. Isn't it true we spend our whole life chasing things? And we are never satisfied, for every time we make a purchase, or achieve a goal, there is the next thing to buy and the next goal to pursue. We chase after cell phones, cars, houses, organic food, clothing, and art. We certainly chase after wealth in order to buy all these things. We chase after accomplishments such as high school and college graduation, marriage, children, vacations, and retirement. We chase after relationships, often from one partner to another, rarely connecting with the one that will complete us, or meet our needs. And so, when one relationship ends, we begin the pursuit of another love who will make our life a bit more fulfilling.

71

It is a simple observation that for the great majority of human beings, life is a journey of chasing things outside of ourselves, in order to make us feel good on the inside. This is what I call living within an Outside In paradigm. It is conditional. Only when the mostly uncontrollable conditions are right, or in place, will someone have a modicum of temporary pleasure, joy, or happiness. This approach requires such a dogged determination, a kind of grind, which ultimately will not lead to any type of sustained self-fulfillment.

This step suggests there is a more powerful way to experience life, an approach more aligned with how things really are, a strategy that will allow you to pursue a happy and healthy life, independent of your life's circumstances, wants, needs and desires. Instead of looking around and chasing things that are outside of yourself, and truly outside of your control, and never fully satisfying, begin to look inside (beliefs, thoughts, feeling, emotions) for your life's satisfaction. This step is an invitation to begin the process of examining and rehabilitating your inner landscape. From this place, the outer adornments will not have the same allure, nor will they define you. You truly are not your smart phone. You are not your car. You are not your clothing. You are certainly not your house or your last European vacation. If you are not any of those things, then who are you? How do you define yourself devoid of a collection of possessions and experiences?

Rather than reacting to your exterior life's circumstances like a puppet on a string, you will become the author of your inner life, free to experience and create in a manner completely in alignment with your own precious and unique spirit. This step invites an experience often referred to as a paradigm shift, one which will allow for more balance, more stillness, more awareness. This step asks you to jump off the merry go round of chasing things to make you happy. And paradoxically, as you do this work, you will find the world will reward you with those outer adornments you no longer need, but can still appreciate and experience with gratitude.

Assignment:

Let's start by shedding some light on our internal landscape. Look at an internal aspect of your life you are not pleased with, or you know could use some work, and describe how this internal aspect manifests outward. For example, you read about how I was ostracized by my schoolmates in 6th grade. This led to a tremendous fear of abandonment. This fear of abandonment (my internal world) manifested in my relationships. I was clingy and overly cloying. I overcompensated for my fear by doing everything I thought I could to keep a woman in my life. As a result, they got tired of my lack of independence and left lickety-split. Write down the main two areas where you can see how your inner world is impacting your outer world. This will give you a few areas to keep in mind as you go through the remaining steps in this book.

Step 12

Know Thyself

"The thing which I think needs to be talked about is at the other end of the spectrum, the barriers to realizing happiness. The barriers to realizing happiness are a lot of very unhappy things. And they are the things which almost nobody talks about because very few of us are willing to confront those things."

—Werner Erhard

Know thyself. It was a shock to me, but in 1999, at the age of 40, I really didn't know anything about myself. This is an excellent example of not knowing about something that I did not know. I thought I was a good guy, but in reality, my dark side was unknown, never looked at, and fairly hideous. I also knew nothing about the dynamics of the triad of ego, self and consciousness. This step will look at both of these topics, our individual self knowledge as well as knowledge of our human condition.

Many of us like to think we are magnificent creatures God can't help but love. We don't like to indulge in those thoughts that make us uncomfortable. We don't want to admit to our competitiveness, and how we hope to be better than everyone else. We'd rather not acknowledge the rage that lives just below the surface. One day in 2000, my day of rainbows and unicorns came to an end. For my entire life up until that time, I believed I was a pretty cool, stand up type of guy. Then, just at the turn of the century, I began a descent into my dark side. When most people hear that phrase, the dark side, they think of something bad. We are conditioned to think that way, aren't we? God is good. The devil is bad. And having the devil in your life, well, that must be very, very bad. But that is not the case. We have it backwards. It is only in embracing our dark side, can we truly become fully integrated human beings.

This is how it all started. I was a student of a very powerful, mystical teacher. He was my only teacher. I had been working with him on and off over an 18 month period. He and I were buddies. We even considered going into business together, wrote up a business plan, and onward we were going to march. Little did I know that this was all a ruse to suck me in to expose all aspects of my dark side. It was truly brilliant. One day in the summer of 2000, after a one-week event in England in which I assisted, he asked me to join him outside in the garden. We sat down to have a chat. After we sat down, very suddenly, he fell over with great force, face first into the dirt. At first I was speechless. Then I asked what had happened and what was the matter? He told me in a voice I barely recognized, "You are doing this to me!" I was dumfounded and at a complete loss. I was scared, for I had no idea what was happening. I helped him up the best I could, trying to understand just what was going on. Then it began. He hit me, hard, very hard, in the chest. I fell backwards, and the next thing I knew he was in my face like no one had ever been in my face before. It didn't even seem like him, but rather an emissary from some other place. And he, or it, kept pounding my chest with his forearm lodged hard across my throat.

Over the next half and hour, he laid out in great detail and supreme authority all of my dark issues in a way I couldn't help but hear and know to be true. He covered all the bases, my arrogance, my predatory sexual thoughts about women, my possessiveness, my unbalanced masculine and feminine energy, my "I'm better than everyone else" energy, my possessiveness, and my sneakiness. By the end of this session, I was sobbing and in a fetal position. I took my teacher's advice, and for the next 3 hours, put dirt on myself and stayed silent in the garden with all that had happened. It was sobering. And it was a new beginning. My life of rock solid steadiness, my life of control, my life of always figuring out what to do, all came to a crumbling halt. It was time to rebuild, with new eyes and a new heart. But the process had only just begun, as there was so much darkness to unearth. I did not know myself at all.

During the next month, another aspect of my dark side became exposed. I began to feel jealous of my wife and her experiences with other men. It was an ungrounded fear of abandonment, that she would find someone better and leave me. I didn't want her to leave me. In fact, the thought of her with another man made me sick to my stomach. I wasn't sleeping well, and I was acting like a real ass. All of this had me feeling depressed and desperate. And that had me feeling angry at my wife, at my teacher, and at my suddenly darkened life. I remember thinking to myself, what did I do to deserve this?

The next aspect of my dark side that I had to face was my arrogance. My family and I were living off our little nest egg in the English countryside. We had all of our money in one place and one man managed all the funds. Well, he turned out to be a thief, and all our money disappeared. Overnight, we were broke. We had to leave England and return to the States in order to begin working again. It was almost as if the universe said to me, "You have to start over, and do it with humbleness and a new appreciation for what you have." Whatever arrogance I had about being better than other people because of my finances crumbled instantaneously. In fact, I had to ask relatives for a loan just so my family and I could get back to the States. Humbling beyond words, yet as I look back, it couldn't have happened any other way.

Once back in the States, my wife clearly had had enough. She tried to support me, but I was unsupportable. And finally, she asked me to leave. And so I left and began a process of living life on my own, without a partner, and without the daily interaction of my children. It was one of the saddest points of my life, no question. And I was unbelievably angry, as well.

The next 2 months, I expressed my anger through words and wrote some poems and letters that grappled with my feelings and my situation. I kept in close contact with many of my male friends who provided tremendous emotional support. The thing that I most noticed, however, was that I was feeling so strong, and so much more masculine energy flowing though me, and all the while I was becoming more aware of everything that was going on around me. My perception increased exponentially. When my friends would have an upsetting issue to share, I knew the answers. It was like, "Dude, I have been there."

In June of 2004, my life took a sharp turn toward nothingness. I don't know why it happened. It was not something I ever saw coming. The universe, in the form of one very powerful woman, whacked me down to the ground, dragged me as if pulled by a car until all my skin was scraped and burned off, and left me reeling. Here was yet another aspect of my dark self for me to experience and embrace

This experience with this woman is all about fire and burning. If you are going to make a real go for a state of enlightenment, you will have to burn. You will have to let go like you have never let go before. Life will be messy. You will have to let go in ways you can't even imagine. It is literally unimaginable. You will have to jump off so many cliffs and free-fall each and every time until you actually get somewhat comfortable with an extreme level of not knowing.

In June of 2004, I was preparing for a 3-day men's initiation weekend event. I was the organizer for the event, a position I held with great pride, and yes, great arrogance. Not many men are willing to commit to putting on such an intense event, nor to deal on a daily basis with the strong women who guide the event and serve as your boss. Now it is a joy. Then however, my ego was not at all copacetic about the relationship.

It must be said at this point that I was a man with questionable integrity. I was a sneak. I was a calculator, always looking at the different angles to any given situation, and then selecting the route that would serve me the best. I thoughts I was clever, oh so clever. Make no mistake about that. I looked like a sincere, selfless male who was doing his bit to serve the good of mankind and be a champion for women. But underneath laid the slithery cold blood of a snake. And to top this all off, I was painfully unaware of this quality of my nature. I was fat and happy and feeling like I was a pretty all right guy.

The week before the event, one of the guides came to my home and spent the week while we began final preparations for the gig. One night we were sitting around the living room table, and the guide began to speak about my lack of integrity. In particular, she spoke directly to my lack of integrity toward her and her organization. She spoke plainly, and said that in her experience, she felt as though I had raped her and the organization by misrepresenting myself with regards to the organization. In fact, she said, I had reenacted the classic male taking from the female that which wasn't his. This hour-long assault had me rocked and reeling. I couldn't help but agree with all that was being said. It was humbling and decimating at the same time. The ground on which I stood had vanished and the free-fall began.

During the ensuing 3-day event, the issue of my integrity came up several times, and each time the fire burned longer and hotter. When one is burning, there really isn't much you can do, other than feel it and acknowledge the truth of the situation. Not only was I burning, I was burning in front of all my male buddies. All these men who seemed to respect me were seeing me get immolated. So while one guide was directing her rage at me, on a larger scale, all the women were raging against all the men. This added a certain and extreme level of fire to the entire event. It was an event few of us will ever forget. It had sharp edges that cut us all.

And in that process, after some time, I moved into forgiveness. It wasn't forgiveness of my wife or God or my teacher, it was forgiveness of myself. Out of that forgiveness came acceptance of all that had happened. I had finally accepted myself, all of myself, light and dark side. As above, so below. I have to say it again; I can be a real bastard.

79

Haven't we all done things, horrible things that we keep stored away in a place that no one else can see? And those things embarrass us and haunt us and shame us only because we don't own them. We think, falsely, that wasn't really me, not the me I know now. It was only through my descent into the dark side, that I came to accept myself, warts and all. And as I work with and meet more men and women, I feel and know the value and the importance of reclaiming our selves, all of our selves, the good, the bad and the ugly.

If we don't own up to all aspects of ourselves, we energetically wear these wounds on our sleeves for all to see. You can't hide them. Isn't it true that you can feel when people aren't being honest with you? You can feel when something isn't being said. You can feel when that sweet person next to you is really a snake. It is only when you delve into the muck that you can resurrect yourself and experience redemption.

I am not the first to say that the height of one's radiance is a function of one's knowing and owning the dark side of ourselves. Ram Dass said it: you can't have the ecstasy without the pain. The deeper the pain, the more profound the bliss. Out of the pain and the relentless struggle comes remarkable clarity and ease. At first it seems a back and forth game. But after a while, you learn to feel the bliss even in the pain. You know that the supreme powers that watch over us are teaching a valuable lesson that you are ready to embrace.

Assignment:

I feel the biggest dark side culprit is low self-esteem. For most, self-loathing is a more accurate assessment of an ongoing internal dialogue. It is there, sort of like a virus that takes over your internal software. With all the weekend events I have participated in, this self-loathing drives many to dysfunction. Again, the key is not to eliminate the self-loathing, but to acknowledge it, accept it, and then begin to dissect it and understand it. The assignment is to ask and answer questions like, when did this self-loathing begin? Or, why do I feel this way about myself? Or, who told me I was less than, or broken, or a failure, or whatever the case may be?

The second part of this assignment is to identify 5 "dark" aspects of your personality. You can start with the 7 deadly sins to get you warmed up: greed, lust, sloth, gluttony, wrath, envy, and pride. In identifying these aspects, we begin the process of learning more about who we are, and healing naturally begins. This knowledge will turn into acceptance and ultimately love.

Step 13

Ego, Self and Consciousness

"With thinking we may be beside ourselves in a sane sense. By a conscious effort of the mind we can stand aloof from actions and their consequences; and all things, good and bad, go by us like a torrent. We are not wholly involved in Nature. I may be either the driftwood in the stream, or Indra in the sky looking down on it. I may be affected by a theatrical exhibition; on the other hand, I may not be affected by an actual event which appears to concern me much more. I only know myself as a human entity; the scene, so to speak, of thoughts and affections; and am sensible of a certain doubleness by which I can stand as remote from myself as from another. However intense my experience, I am conscious of the presence and criticism of a part of me, which, as it were, is not a part of me, but spectator, sharing no experience, but taking note of it, and that is no more I than it is you. When the play, it may be the tragedy, of life is over, the spectator goes his way. It was a kind of fiction, a work of the imagination only, so far as he was concerned."

—Henry David Thoreau

If we are truly going to embark on a life of radical freedom, we must understand the basic components of the human condition. Until we are able to first understand, and then work with the various components, we are naïve and ineffective at self-transformation. One of the reasons the practice of meditation is such a powerful discipline is it allows us to slow down the ego mechanism and expose the less vociferous elements of our being. This breakdown of the mind should not be believed on face value. Think for yourself about how it is in your own mind. Question my assertions here, for it is vitally important that you see and understand and comprehend the significance of this triad relationship. Let's meet the characters.

Let's start with the loudest, which is ego. Ego believes the squeaky wheel gets the grease. The great majority of the world population most closely identifies with the ego, and assumes this is who they are. The ego is the loudest voice in our head, the voice with opinions, the voice with fears, the voice with a penchant for comfort and the status quo. The ego does not like to rock the boat, burn the boats, jump of the cliff, go for it, nor be quiet. The ego would like you to believe he or she is you, and if not you, then your best friend. It is important to state here that the ego is not an enemy. You can't get rid of the ego. You and your ego will be connected until the day of your final breath. The goal is not to destroy the ego, but rather understand the ego, and be able to quiet the ego from time to time and ultimately to quiet it for longer and longer periods of time.

Knowledge of the ego's tactics is of primary importance. If you don't recognize what the ego is doing, then you will fall victim to its manipulations. So let's talk about the ego's tactics. First, know that the ego does not like change. It does not like the unknown. The ego prefers comfort and stability and the status quo. Do you know how your mind starts to race when you take on a big project, or you agree to a deadline, or you find yourself in a room with strangers, that is the ego reacting to change, gently whispering in your ear at first, and the bellowing aloud that what you are doing is not such a good idea. Better we go back home, the ego says, and watch that movie we have on our computer, or dash out for an In N Out burger, or do anything besides this uncomfortable stuff. You will have to listen, but how will you respond? The choice is yours, grow and expand, or shrink and return to comfort. That is often the choice. If you don't understand how ego works, and don't recognize it simply as a voice that wants to share, then it is difficult to say no. But now you know it is just a loud voice that may not have your biggest and best interests at heart, therefore you are in a much better position to make a considered decision.

Let's meet the second character that constitutes our conscious being, and that is the self, or the one that listens and observes. Haven't you ever wondered, with all the chattering going on inside your head, who is listening? Your true self listens. Your true self is the final arbiter of your actions. Your true self is judge and jury and shapes every moment of your life. Your true self is who you need to get to know better. For most, the true self is drowned out by all the noise. When listened to, your true self opens up your world to your intuition, your sixth sense, your magic, your synchronicity and your awakening.

In speaking about these two characters that live within us, the name of Ego or False Self has been assigned to the speaker, and the name of True Self or No Self has been assigned to the listener. In the general process of slowing life down, and in the specific process of meditating, the dynamics of the Ego and True Self become self-evident. Isn't it remarkable that this dynamic is so rarely talked about? It is not taught in school. It is as if it does not exist. Yet we all are built with this inherent relationship between a speaker and a listener. I am a big fan of the Matrix trilogy of movies. In the first movie, we are exposed to a Latin phrase, "Temet Nosce," which means Know Thyself. This awareness of the Ego/False Self and the Listener/True Self is essential self-knowledge in the pursuit of a simpler and more serene life.

The more I began to meditate, the easier it was for me to detach from the activities in my life. Detachment does not mean I lived my life any less fully. It was quite the contrary. Rather, it means I was able to be still in the face of life instead of being reactionary. There is a big difference between reacting to the ego's ministrations (no choice) and responding to life (self knowledge and choice), which we cover in greater detail later in the book.

Meditate, become more sensitive, and take it as a criterion that you will go on becoming more and more detached. If you feel that attachment is growing, then you are erring somewhere in your meditation. These are the criteria. And to me, attachment cannot be destroyed and detachment cannot be practiced. You can only practice meditation – and detachment will follow as a consequence, as a by-product. If meditation really flowers within you, you will have a feeling of detachment. Then you can move anywhere and you will remain untouched, unafraid.

—Osho.

The chart at the end of this step clearly makes the distinction between the Ego/False Self and the Observer/True Self. As you look at the chart, it becomes apparent which side of the ledger we'd all choose. This is the beautiful result of a consistent meditation practice. Not only does one feel better, but one also begins to experience a greater understanding of the underpinnings of being a human being. In that understanding lives truth. In that understanding lives an awakening. In that understanding lives a pure and natural synchronicity with life itself. In that understanding lives radical freedom from the pernicious whisperings of the ego.

"The soul's communication of truth is the highest event in nature... and this communication is an influx of the Divine Mind into our mind... Every moment when the individual feels invaded by it is memorable."

—Ralph Waldo Emerson

The third element, which isn't really a human element, yet is an element we can invite into our lives, is spirit, or consciousness. Emerson refers to spirit in his quote as Divine Mind. The more we can become still, and the more we can quiet the ego, the more we can invite and be witness to spirit as it flows through us. In my workshops, I refer to human beings as portals. We literally are the gates of heaven, and we can open up for business, or keep the gates closed as a result of ignorance, unwillingness, or forgetfulness. As you become more adept at slowing life down and stopping the world and holding that open and freeing space for spirit to flow, you will start to recognize the unique, creative and unpredictable nature of spirit. You will also marvel at the beautiful brilliance of the universal energy flowing through. In Native American lore, we hear the concept of the Hollow Bone, referring to a bone that has ample space for spirit to flow. Indeed.

When we begin to make these distinctions, the truth of our nature is undeniable. We are neither ego, nor true self. We are pure consciousness. We always have been and always will be. This is a very liberating realization. This step invites you to begin the process of understanding the dynamics of you. Who are you really? This is a

86

question that demands our full attention.

Assignment:

Undertake to do the Dome meditation. The following mediation is useful and supportive in the process of making the distinction between the false self, the true self and consciousness. Read it over, and then during your meditation, begin to play with the relationship between the two components. Enjoy.

The Dome Meditation: Read through these instructions a few times so that you can close your eyes and proceed through the meditation to the end.

Let's now begin to experience the Ego in comparison to the True Self.

Imagine the listener first, and see it as a big dome, like a movie theatre.

There is no real listener. Rather, if you can begin to experience the listener as a portal through which words flow.

Most of the words that go through the portal are the words of your ego: talk, talk, talk.

See the words like a billboard in front of you.

Try it with, "I am meditating right now."

Say it to yourself, and see those words flow by on the billboard.

This is the process. This is the discipline. Have conscious awareness of the words flowing through the portal.

Now try it and remove the billboard. Watch the words flow by, floating on air, right in front of you, present in the dome.

This is the discipline. The ego will not like this. It does not like being observed as simple automated machinery, but that is all that it is. Your ego is a machine. You can't stop it. The words will keep on flowing by.

Continue to observe the words floating by.

Try it now with, "My ego is just a machine I do not fully understand yet." Watch those words float by. Any thoughts, watch them as words floating by. Nothing right about the words. Nothing wrong about the words. They are only words, and they are not you.

Now put your attention on the dome.

Allow yourself to fully inhabit the dome. Imagine you are nothing but space, the space that inhabits not only the dome, but every place imaginable.

If it helps you, imagine you are floating in deep blue space. No body, but pure consciousness floating freely, no fear, no thinking, no self-consciousness, just there observing all there is, all there ever was, and all there will ever be. Begin to see everything in terms of infinity.

Now return to the dome.

Watch the mechanism of the ego machine. Disarm the Ego and simply watch the words float by. Notice how the thinking just happens. No stopping it. Let the words flow. Watch the words.

The Ego will want to take credit for your discoveries. Your Ego is like the fox guarding the hen house. Thank it for sharing.

*****

This is something you can try once you have done the Dome meditation a few times:

I have developed a simple energy exercise that serves to accelerate the process of experiencing grace. It is a combination of two different guided meditations that when combined, work to blank the mind of thought and allows for a sense of grace to descend upon you. If you don't know anything about chakras, do an Internet search so you are at least familiar with the nature of chakras and associated colors.

Begin by meditating quietly for about 10 minutes, or until your mind stops chattering vociferously at you. Then do the dome meditation. Once you are in a settled place, imagine your crown chakra fully open, violet and receptive. Then, on your in breath, see your crown chakra pierce into the bottom of the dome, and continue through and out the top. Then on the out breath, pull in the grace, the divinity, and allow it to settle in your heart. Do this for about ten breaths, and then stop. This process produces a powerful experience of grace. My crown gets very warm, and I feel a strong vibration in my heart chakra. Try it out and see what you get.

EGO / FALSE SELF ⟷	LISTENER / TRUE SELF
You / Them	Me / Us
Fear Based	Awareness Based
Separation	Unity
Duality	Oneness
Finite	Infinite
Grasps at Security	Embraces Vulnerability
Constant / Relentless Tension	Ease of Being
Self Importance / Pride	Generosity of Spirit
Must Plan and Control	All In Right Timing
Blame	Understanding
Hostility	Love
Resentment	Forgiveness
Complain	Gratefull
Reactive	Responsive
Territorial	Non - Possesive
Thrives on Drama	Enjoys the flow of life
Jelousy	Co - Existence
Anger	Happiness
Demands to be heard	Finds Serenity in Silence
Lies to you	Shares Wisdom
Power	Humility
Materialism	Spiritualism
Insanity	Wisdom
War	Peace
Coldness	Sympathy / Compassion
Past / Future Oriented	Now Oriented
Intolerant	Accepting
Egoism	Altruism
Self - Denial	Self Acceptance
Social Intolerance	Social Acceptance
Living up to expectations	Simplicity
Doing	Being

Step 14

Raising Energy

"The trick to money is having some. If you raise your energy people will be pulled to you, when they show up, bill 'em."

—Stuart Wilde

In the confronting of our self, we become aware. As our awareness grows, the level of our energy rises up. It is this process of raising our energy that at times can feel like an exuberant shot of adrenalin. Raising our energy is also a symptom of a simpler life. With less internal chatter, there is more room for pure energy to live. The process of not only accepting who we are, but also of understanding who we are, leads to a higher internal vibration. This higher vibration is very attractive. The good things in life rest in the realm of higher vibrations. Money is energy. If you want more money, raise your energy. Love is energy. If you want more love, raise your energy. Do the work in this book, and you will immediately feel a shift, and you will notice the world responds to you in a different and wonderful way. Of course, the world hasn't transformed; you will have transformed, and by shifting your context, the world becomes softer and gentler. More and more people become generous and friendly. But it all begins with you.

In the process of going within, one is forced to confront all aspects of him or her self. For each of us, there are some great qualities we possess, and there are some not so wonderful qualities as well. In all cases, that which is our greatest gift will also be our greatest weakness. For example, a man may be particularly loving and giving to his family, while at the same time being too generous in his work life, which results in his being overlooked for promotions. A woman may be unusually passionate in a relationship, while also being far too quick to anger in other situations. It is only in the awareness of our strengths and weaknesses that healing may occur so our lives may improve.

"You can search throughout the entire universe for someone who is more deserving of your love and affection than you are yourself, and that person is not to be found anywhere. You yourself, as much as anybody in the entire universe deserve your love and affection."

—Buddha

We all do stupid things. We hurt people. People hurt us. For some, our parents told us we weren't any good. On and on, there are so many reasons people feel bad about being exactly who they are. It is an epidemic. It lies deep, and most don't ever want to go that deep for fear of how they may feel. Certainly it is more comfortable to cover those feelings up and just move on. Ignorance is bliss, but not really. Fully knowing yourself is the real bliss. Walking the Earth without fear of fear is bliss. Walking the earth knowing you know yourself is bliss. Walking the earth knowing what is true, now that is bliss. Why sell yourself short?

Several of the steps in this book put an emphasis on ways you can raise your energy. You can't expect to live a life of radical freedom while your energy is low and slow and hovering in those darker realms. Many of the steps in this book will serve to raise your energy. Learning how to breathe properly, developing a meditation practice, creating a circle of like-minded friends, exercise, getting adequate sleep, reducing the amount of technology you consume, reducing stress and engaging in a challenge, all of these opportunities will raise your energy.

As Stuart Wilde's quote points out, as you raise your energy, you then have something of value to offer the world. You will need to figure out how to express the energy. However, rather than being an energy vampire, you will have loads of fresh positive energy to share. People will pay for an expression of that, if you have a way to bill them. Why do some people have a world of abundance, and others struggle? The abundant folks have two things: a way to express their energy, and a way to get paid for it. You need both if you want to experience financial freedom, which is an essential part of radical freedom. Without money, in our culture, you can't be too free. If you can't jump on a plane and visit your mate in Madagascar because you don't have the funds, you aren't free. You are grounded. Let's continue working on getting free.

Look around you at the people in your life. Begin to notice who is running on a fairly clean energy system, and who is running on a clogged up energy system. It is easy to see once you begin to notice the dynamics. The invitation is to make a concerted effort to surround yourself with people who are aware and who display strong, vibrant and healthy energy. By the simple laws of physics, you will begin to experience a heightening of your own energy by the company you keep. You can have friends who raise your energy, or lower your energy. It may seem brutal to drop some of your friends who are dragging you down, but the life you are improving is yours. And think of all the cool people you are going to meet. Think about all the lessons you will learn. Think about how amazing this life can be when your energy is high, and you truly begin to know yourself.

Here is an example of someone who is an absolute A-lister in my book. Mon is a beautiful woman, mid 40s, who currently works two jobs. Morning job is running a restaurant. Evening job is serving drinks and running a bar. I met Mon on my first bar visit in Chiang Mai several months ago. She brought me my Singha beer, and we played a game called Get Four. Hanging out with Mon continues to be a joy. She has a big spirit and infectious smile. She has a teenage boy, and also adopted a now two-year-old girl. Let's return to the first night I met Mon at Wayne's World Bar.

Four beers after arriving, and 5 straight losses at the game, Mon told me she would be opening her own bar, and it would be called Moon

Bar. She told me about the sign for the bar, and I told her my ideas. I drew it out on a piece of paper, and she loved it. I subsequently took a few minutes and created the logo in Photoshop and texted it to her. Soon her sign will be up, and Mon will be operating her very own bar. Two jobs, two children, single mom, you have to respect her work ethic.

This is what I want to share. Mon is very popular with all the girls that work at Wayne's bar. She appears to me to be a matriarchal figure. She is about 20 years older than most of them, and she has seen quite a bit of life. So the other night I said, "Mon, are you taking any of the girls over to the new bar with you?" Without a thought, Mon said "No, not good for Wayne. No good for him, no good for me."

I think it is fair to say that most people would not take that same position. Most people would be looking out for themselves first, and let Wayne figure it out on his own. Even though these women are friends of Mon's first, she inherently knows that doing the right thing is the best thing in the long run for both her and Wayne. Perhaps it is the Buddhist belief in Karma, which informs Mon's life philosophy. I don't know. I do know that when she answered my question, I knew she was right on so many levels. Her response was so simple, so concise, so integrous and so pure. I have been in the position of starting my own businesses in the past. I did not always operate with "Mon quality" integrity. I suffered because of it. "No good for him, no good for me." That is something I feel is worth remembering. This is something that will keep your energy running high and clean and unencumbered.

Another powerful way to raise your energy is to challenge yourself. What is it that you most want right now? I have challenged myself to lose a certain amount of weight over a 90-day period. I have challenged myself to achieve a lotus position in yoga over a 90-day period. Right now I am in a challenge to complete this book in the next 30 days. Challenges put a fire in your belly. Challenges put your focus on something you have determined has great value for you.

Challenges put you at your edge. Challenges raise your energy as a natural response to your commitment. There are a few basic rules to adhere to when setting up a challenge. First, write your goal down. Second, be specific about your intended results, and your time frame. Third, tell five people whom you can count on to hold you accountable. Do that and watch your energy rise. Up and up we go.

Assignment:

Your assignment is two-fold. Create a list of 5 people who will constitute your inner circle. Reach out to each one of them. You may need to stop interacting with some of your current inner circle mates. If you have difficulty with this, always go back to your vision. Have a clear image in your head of what you want in your life. Who are the people who will help you to get there, and who is standing in your way?

The second assignment is to declare and begin a 30-day (could be longer, but not shorter) challenge. Share this with your inner circle. I would also suggest sharing it on social media, as you will get quite a bit of positive reinforcement. Then begin your challenge.

Step 15

Tool Kit

"Men are not prisoners of fate, but prisoners of their own minds."

—Franklin D. Roosevelt

It is interesting to me that people will spend a great deal of time cleaning their room, or their house, their car, or weeding their garden, yet don't give much consideration to the thoughts that are floating around in their head. Of all the things that deserve your primary focus, and your best weeding and cleaning effort, the thoughts you entertain and give energy to should be at the top of your list. Would you rather pull a weed out of your tomato garden at home, or pull a nasty pernicious thought out of the mental toolkit of your mind? Think of your mindset like a tool kit. Most of us have been carrying around tools that at one time helped us out, but now no longer serve us.

The more you practice a meditation discipline, the more detached you will become from your thoughts. You will be able to observe them, evaluate them, and focus your energy on the thoughts that empower you, and for the ones that cause you harm, let them be. Stop watering them and let them die of their own accord. I invite you to review the list of deleterious thoughts, and make a note of which ones you are still entertaining as truth.

- Too many people are smarter than me.

- My parents didn't do enough for me.

97

- I'm a slow learner.

- My partner isn't supportive enough.

- I'm comfortable doing what I'm doing now.

- I would fail for sure if I tried that.

- I'm really stupid when it comes to X.

- I make too many mistakes when I try something new.

- Taking risks always turns out bad for me.

- The way I have operated in the past works well enough.

- I'm comfortable doing what I'm doing now.

- Successful people are just lucky.

- I deserve better.

- I work very hard, isn't that enough?

- I'm a failure.

- I would fail for sure if I tried that.

- I'm really stupid when it comes to X.

- I make too many mistakes when I try something new.

- Taking risks always turns out bad for me.

- The way I have operated in the past works well enough.

- I am past my prime. It's too late for me.

- I will never find love. That's for other people.

That is a good list. How many did you read and think to yourself, yep, I feel that way? You can't eliminate thoughts. They rise and fall randomly. There is nothing you can do about that. But what you can do is observe. You can notice how some of these thoughts are powerful and persistent. Most importantly, you can stop feeding these thoughts one more smidge of energy. You can, essentially, starve them out. Thoughts like these require your energy to exist. If you stop feeding them energy, they will slowly die off. This is the practice, to create a growing awareness of the machinations of the mind. In that observation, you will see just how asleep at the wheel you may have been. Time to wake up, clean the attic, and maintain a tool kit of positive and empowering thoughts. Try these on for size:

I am amazing

When I commit to something, I am a success.

I am determined to be free.

I deserve freedom as much as anyone.

I will work hard so that I may have time off without guilt.

I will meditate so as to better understand myself and my fellow man/woman.

I am growing as a person and it feels fantastic.

The world is a safe place.

I will take risks when my intuition tells me the time is right.

I trust my sixth sense to guide me.

The universe has my back.

The Dude abides.

Assignment:

Your assignment is to come up with 5 positive thoughts you can carry around with you and play in your mind throughout the day. How glorious it is to create your own operating system, your own toolkit of thoughts, and then watch how the world shows up for you. Does this mean all the harmful thoughts will just go away? No, but as they notice you aren't feeding them any energy, and instead, the new kids on the block are getting all the attention, slowly they will fade away. Devil be gone!

Step 16

The Power of Music

"Oh let the sun beat down upon my face
With stars to fill my dream.
I am a traveler of both time and space
To be where I have been. "

—Kashmir by Led Zeppelin

A musical interlude....

I do quite a bit of writing. The truth about writing to which most authors will readily admit is it is often a laborious chore. Sure, there are times in which a rich wave of inspiration hits, and the words freely flow out of your fingertips on to the keyboard and are then made real on the screen, but that is rare. Instead, I sit down at the same time each day, usually in the same spot, although I do mix it up when I can and sit in a coffee shop or restaurant, and I look at a blank screen. This scenario is just the beginning. This is where the work begins. Inspired or not, I will start to type.

One thing that I do which supports me in my writing is to combine my love of music with my writing time. Some writers need complete silence. I do not. Music is a catalyst for my emotions. Music brings up memories. Music makes me happy. Ever since I heard Stairway to Heaven by Led Zeppelin back in high school, I knew music would be a part of my life. Make no mistake, I am not a musician. I can't sing, and don't play an instrument. But let me listen to 28 minutes of Dazed and Confused and nine times out of ten I will have tears in my eyes during the guitar solos. Music touches my soul.

Over the past year, I have been creating a playlist in ITunes entitled "AA – Writing Music." The first thing I did was add a few artists that I knew belonged on the list: Van Morrison. Miles Davis, Radiohead, Bob (Marley and Dylan), Leonard Cohen and Keith Jarrett. I had seen Keith Jarrett in concert several times in my twenties. He is such a unique performer, improvising the entire concert. He needed absolute silence or else he would either yell at the protagonist, or refuse to perform. In addition to his virtuoso piano playing, he would also vocalize a bit, working with everything he had to get the most out of himself and his instrument. I remember feeling grateful to experience such brave and marvelous performances.

Now, decades later, as I look at the blank screen, I often think of Keith Jarrett in front of thousands, with a blank canvas in front of him, creating something from nothing. When I hear his Koln Concert performance in my earphones, I am inspired. What one man can do, another can do. Now as I write, I hear the music of some of my all time greats playing and some new artists too. The list continues to evolve. I recently added an Irish musician Hozier and the new CD by Annie Lennox. Writing has become less of a chore, for it is now also an opportunity to do something I love which is to listen to music. As I write this, a live version of John Coltrane's Naima is playing. I am off into my own little world with all my writing and musician buddies. How amazing this life is!

Assignment:

This should be fun. Create a playlist of music that inspires you. You can find just about any song on YouTube. Listen to the oldies. Listen to some contemporary tunes as well. What moves you? What songs can support you in reaching your goals? Select a minimum of 10 songs.

Step 17

Managing Stress

"We must have a pie. Stress cannot exist in the presence of a pie."

— David Mamet

Not too long ago, I was going through a divorce after nearly 20 years of marriage. I had moved out of my house, and away from my then 15-year-old daughter, in order to keep a semblance of peace in the family. I had recently made a job change, and it had turned out to be my lowest paying position during the last 30 years. These are some major life stressors: end of a relationship, job change, financial concerns, and not seeing my daughter. When life hits, it hits hard.

I share all of this so you know I understand something about stress. And don't we all? As a result of these life events, I have had to go to some deep places to find serenity. I have tried quite a wide range of healing modalities (diets, exercise routines, hot saunas, sweat lodges, yoga, meditation, nature walks, ayahuasca, ecstasy, workshops and rage release, to name just a few), and refined my approach based on my real life experiences.

Let's start off by looking at what life is for so many of us and how stress impacts us. I will find little argument when I say the sources of stress are everywhere: work, relationships, information overload, children, noise, pollution, violence, over-population, extinction, confusion, competition. And these are just a few first world problems. In other parts of the world malaria, the Ebola virus, dirty drinking water, little or no education opportunity and hunger exist to keep human beings in a constant state of tension and stress. It is different now than it was for our caveman brothers and sisters who had two main stressors, find food to eat and don't become someone else's food to eat. We have a whole new level of complexity.

What is stress? Stress is pressure or tension exerted on a material object. Therefore, there are two components to stress: the thing doing the stressing, and the thing receiving the stress. Therefore, There are two ways to reduce stress. One is to reduce the pressure from the external object. This is an important distinction. The stressors will continue if not exacerbate over time. Rarely do we have any control over the external forces. For example, if you are in an abusive relationship, or you have a very demanding boss at work, you can walk away from the stress. Get out of there. Still, there are far too many things that cause stress that cannot be eliminated. The second and more reliable approach is to work on ourselves to become more pliable, more flexible, more resilient, and more knowledgeable.

The reason I emphasize the nature of stress is because stress is the silent killer of our time. Not only does it literally kill us, but if you are constantly stressed out, there is absolutely no way you are going to achieve any long lasting freedom. Let's look at some alarming statistics.

*7 out of every 10 people who die each year had been living with a chronic illness.

*1 out of every 2 of us is now living with a chronic illness.

*For 3 of every 4 of those with a chronic illness, STRESS may be a contributing factor.

(American Medical Association)

*A full 43% of US adults suffer adverse effects from STRESS.

(American Psychological Association)

*More than 80% of physician office visits are associated with unresolved stress issues.

*Stress is a big factor in more than 75% of all illnesses diagnosed today with many studies putting this figure closer to 90%.

(www.About.com)

*Depression, only one type of stress reaction, is predicted to be the leading occupational disease of the 21st century, responsible for more days lost than any other single factor.

*$300 Billion, or $7,500 per employee, is spent annually in the US on stress-related compensation claims, reduced productivity, absenteeism, health insurance costs, direct medical expenses (nearly 50% higher for workers who report stress), and employee turnover.

(www.stressdirections.com)

30% of tweens and 42% of teens say they get headaches. However, only 13% of parents reported being aware of their children having headaches.

39% of tweens and 49% of teens report difficulty sleeping. However, only 13% of parents reported being aware of their children having trouble sleeping.

25% of tweens and 39% of teens reported eating too much or too little due to stress. However, only 8% of parents reported being aware of this issue.

All of the above stress statistics related to children and their parents were reported by a 2009 survey conducted by the American Psychological Association (APA).

45% of workers report that job insecurity has a significant impact on stress levels.

61% of workers list heavy workloads as a significant impact on stress levels.

25% of workers have taken a mental health day to cope with stress.

54% of workers are concerned about health problems due to stress.

All of the above statistics related to work stress were reported by a 2004 survey conducted by the APA.

40% of workers report that their job is "very or extremely" stressful.

25% of workers view their jobs as the number one stressor in their lives.

Survey by Northwestern National Live

26% of workers report they are "often or very often burned out or stressed by their work."

Survey by the Families and Work Institute

29% of workers report they feel "quite a bit or extremely stressed at work."

Survey by Yale University

The Following stress statistics are from surveys conducted by the APA:

54% of Americans are concerned about the level of stress in their everyday lives. (2004)

75% of adults reported experiencing moderate to high levels of stress in the past month. (2009)

42% of adults reported that their stress has increased in the past year. (2009)

The following statistics are from a 2009 survey conducted by the APA where during the previous month many adults reported feeling the following physical effects of stress:

47% report lying awake at night

45% report irritability or anger

43% report fatigue

40% report lack of Interest, motivation or energy

34% report headaches

34% report feeling sad or depressed

32% report feeling as though they could cry

27% report upset stomach or indigestion

How do we deal with stress?

56% of women and 40% of men reported eating poorly

43% of women and 32% of men reported napping

25% of women and 11% of men reported shopping

18% reported drinking alcohol

16% reported smoking

When we're stressed, it's not uncommon to lie down at night and replay our problems over and over in our heads. One of the worst parts of this symptom is that it creates a vicious cycle. The more sleep deprived we are, the less we are able to deal with stressful situations and life in general. And then in turn, the more stressed we are, the less restful sleep we are sometimes able to get.

Many people overeat when their emotions are out of whack. It's common for people to deal with stressful or emotional situations by eating more than usual. However, it's also common for people to eat less or not at all during these times. Sometimes stress can cause nausea, heartburn, indigestion, diarrhea, constipation, or even ulcers. Physical symptoms are not the only ways stress can present itself. Be on the lookout for mental or emotional symptoms as well. Stress often leads to anger, depression, irritability, uncontrollable crying, mood swings, anxiety, nervousness and restlessness.

These are fairly alarming, dare I say stressful, statistics. If you are like me, you can recognize yourself in some of those figures. I find that reading statistics on stress is damned stressful. However, if we are to make any progress, we must accurately assess the situation. To quote Rumi, "The elixir is in the poison!" What that means is that we can only find solutions by thoroughly investigating the problem.

The biggest lesson I have learned is that stress, in general, comes from a feeling of being out of control. Therefore, a common mistake many people make (see the statistics above) is to try to control everything. Trying to control everything is just another way to create stress. Why? There are too many things in life we can't control.

Let's reposition stress as a reaction to the things we come across every day that we can't control. Our reaction to the things we can't control is something we can control. In other words, we can work on our internal dialogue, change some behaviors, and alter how we look at the world, all in an orchestrated effort to create a solid grounded place from which we can respond (rather than react) to life's stressful activities. Reacting only makes you a victim of your life. Being a victim is stressful. Responding gives you creative authorship of your life. Being the author of your life is empowering.

To properly managing stress is to properly manage you. Global warming, relationship struggles, and crying babies are not going to stop. Learning how to be so those experiences are not so stressful, well, that is worth pursuing. A life of little or no stress leads to an awakening to a reality of abundance and joy and of knowing that everything is happening just as it should. You will feel far more freedom to take powerful action without debilitating fear, while experiencing a lightness and authentic joy. Bring it on!

Assignment:

Here are a few exercises to begin the process of stress reduction:

1. Take 5 minutes and write down all the things you can think of that cause you stress. Just keep writing until you are done. Don't be afraid to write it all down. It must be written on a piece of paper. Don't type it up on a computer.

2. Write down all the people who cause you stress. Especially look back at your family and friend relationships. Write them all down.

3. Acknowledge that some of these people and situations can be changed. Change them as you see fit. Others can not immediately be eliminated. What changes can you make within yourself so that these people and situation, while being stressful, do not cause you stress?

4. Eat some pie!

Step 18

The Pen

"If I don't write to empty my mind, I go mad."

—Lord Byron

As I write this, I am sitting on a bed in Phuket, Thailand. My trusty MacBook Pro is on my lap while Thailand's famous monsoon season roars outside. I am staying in a house one mile from Bangtao Beach. Thailand will be my home for the next 6 months or so as I explore the world and experience new cultures and people. I look out my windows and see mostly trees and mountains. A bird flies across the horizon. Last night, the sound of rain and thunder woke me up several times. I felt like Dorothy in *The Wizard of Oz* as her house was lifted to the sky. The clouds today have that plump grey look about them, and the rainy season is firmly upon us. I have a hot cup of coffee in my big white mug by my side on the nightstand. Incense is burning and a candle is ablaze. I am listening to the latest Leonard Cohen download, along with a mix of jazz, blues, and Gregorian chant. For the next two hours, I will write. I could not be more content.

The remainder of this step is all about the importance of writing things down. Earlier, we discussed the value of meditating as a way to not only slow things down a bit, but also to give us an insight into the nature of our existence. Well, writing is simply another tool we have at our disposal to continue the process of slowing things down, and also supporting us in further understanding how we operate in the world, and how we might be able to further embody peace and serenity. The process of writing also allows us to perform a "mind dump," thereby taking our thoughts out of our head, and putting them down on paper. Writing is an effective way to stop us from compulsive thinking, while allowing some room for our intuition to play a more significant role in our life.

We live in an information heavy world. With the advent of the personal computer, the Internet, and now smartphones, we have a ridiculous amount of information literally at our fingertips. On the one hand, this is such an amazing time to be alive. For example, I can be hungry for a hamburger, pop open an app, look at pictures of hamburgers, read reviews of hamburger joints wherever I might be, see which has the highest customer rating, then put the address into a GPS app, and follow the directions to my next meal. Wow! That is amazing. And the hamburger and onion rings and chocolate malt (must be made with vanilla ice cream) were phenomenal.

The downside of all this information is that it can all be a bit daunting, and frankly, overwhelming. I could easily spend an hour or more per day on Facebook. I could easily spend several hours watching cable news. And by the time I finished consuming all this information, there would be still more new information that needs consuming. It is impossible to keep up! Then throw in about 50 texts and 20 phone calls and several hundred emails, and mix in a nice batch of Words with Friends or Angry Birds, and before you know it, our minds are completely full with information.

A university professor went to visit a famous Zen master. While the master quietly served tea, the professor talked about Zen. The master poured the visitor's cup to the brim, and then kept pouring. The professor watched the overflowing cup until he could no longer restrain himself. "It's overfull! No more will go in!" the professor blurted. "You are like this cup," the master replied. "How can I show you Zen unless you first empty your cup."

The discipline of writing is the act of emptying your cup. Something powerful happens when you take your thoughts and put them down on paper. Not only do you give your mind a bit of breathing room, but you also allow yourself the opportunity to be more objective about what you put on paper (or on the computer screen, as is more often the case). By putting the words on the page, you can then start to inquire into the fundamental qualities of the thought. We need an example.

During one of our weekend initiation events, we do a process called the Yellow and Blue Process. It is really simple. On a yellow piece of paper, we write down the three things we did that causes us the most shame. On the blue piece of paper, we write down the three things that were done to us that cause us the most shame. We then share these items with the group. It is remarkable how much stuff we carry around, for a lifetime, without sharing it and/or releasing it. I have seen men trembling with fear and embarrassment while sharing the most innocent of experiences. It appears much of this shameful stuff happens just around 6th grade! Just the speaking of the incidents is, in most case, a massive life affirming relief. Being heard and understanding that we are not alone, and that we are still loved even after admitting to such things, is purely and positively transformational. At the end of the process, each man is invited to throw the yellow and blue pieces of paper into a fire, and experience a release from the shame.

The actions of writing down some of our life experiences takes the experience out of our head, where it seems to do little good, and places it in front of us to examine, and consider, and take more appropriate action. If our minds are full, as the Zen teacher is suggesting, then there is no room for anything of substance that can serve us in our search for more peace and serenity. For most of my adult life, I have been aware of the truth of this statement: "I don't know what I don't know." That is a powerful realization. Writing is a tool we can all use to open up some room for those things, those concepts, those nuggets, those aha moments, that we do not now know.

During all of our weekend events, one of the first things we do is give each person a journal. Each journal we hand out is unique so that each person can have a feeling of a special relationship with his book. This special relationship with a journal seems to inspire more heartfelt writing. Men tend to have a harder time expressing themselves, and particularly expressing their feelings. Therefore, the discipline of writing also begins to break up that resistance to full self-expression. Writing allows all of us to say what we need to say, say everything we need to say, and begin to discover a voice for what we have to say.

The other significant benefit of writing is the discipline of self-expression. If you feel uncomfortable verbally expressing yourself in a public arena, writing is a marvelous way to begin the process of finding your voice. As you write, so you begin to speak. The pen truly is mightier than the sword. In this day and age, most of us use a laptop rather than a pen. The keyboard is mightier than the Taser. You have a story to tell. Share. Be generous with your life. Let part of it go. Flex those self-expression muscles. Let's get to it.

Assignment:

Oftentimes, our voice is so reactionary; the only expression we allow ourselves is anger. Let's take this opportunity to do just a bit of writing. Let's delve into anger. The first thing we will do is sit still for a few minutes, close our eyes, and think about the one thing, or person, or incident, that generates the most anger in us. Once you have that thing, person, or incident identified, open your eyes, get a journal or piece of paper, and write it down. Notice how you feel writing it down. If you are like me, you will begin to notice the slightest bit of release, a subtle sense of authorship over the situation, and a feeling of contentment for taking some control.

Next, we will use this opportunity to flesh out all the feelings, emotions, and sensations associated with this item (thing, person, or incident). Take just a minute for each of these questions, and write down the answers as you feel them. There is no right or wrong answer. The point of this exercise to get more familiar with your feelings, and to get this information out of your head and onto the piece of paper.

What sensations are associated with your item?

What perceptions are associated with your item?

What thoughts are associated with your item?

What feelings are associated with your item?

What emotions are associated with your item?

What attitudes are associated with your item?

What points of view are associated with your item?

What mental states are associated with your item?

What considerations are associated with your item?

What evaluations are associated with your item?

What judgments are associated with your item?

What images from the past are associated with your item?

Are there any other memories associate with your item?

Upon completing this process, you should have a much greater understanding of the situation of which you were writing. For most, this process creates a remarkable feeling of being unburdened. For some, all of the reactionary energy actually disappears and is replaced with a lightness of being that can only be described as miraculous. This is the power and magic of writing. Lord Byron was on to something!

Step 19

Physical Discipline

"In essence, if we want to direct our lives, we must take control of our consistent actions. It's not what we do once in a while that shapes our lives, but what we do consistently."

— Anthony Robbins

One day a handful of people were on a small boat with Richard Branson heading out to his private island, Necker Island, for a few days. One of the guys on the boat asked something along the lines of, "Richard, how can I be more productive?" Keep in mind, Richard is the founder and operator of a 400-company conglomerate. He also has dyslexia and a poor academic track record. His accomplishments in the business world are legendary. From space travel to deep-sea exploration, to music and cell phones, Richard Branson, at the age of 61, has created an amazing life of abundance and creativity.

Hence, the crowd of boat passengers hung on the edge of their seat cushions in anticipation of what turned out to be an unbelievably simple answer...

Richard responded, "Work out."

That was it.

And that has turned out to be the answer to so many seemingly 'hard' to solve problems:

- How do I get more energy? Work out.

- How do I get more confidence? Work out.

- How do I keep from getting sick? Work out.

- How do I find more time? Work out.

- How do I stay focused? Work out.

- How do I look and feel better?

Taking care of your physical body, the temple of your spirit, is a sure fire way to maintain a consistent level of energy. Richard Branson tells us it is the most important thing you can do to improve your productivity. When I am not careful about the food I put in my body, when I stop exercising, or when I don't get enough sleep, I simply can't operate and maintain a top level of energy. My body can't do it without care and attention.

I am not an expert in any of these fields, but I do have quite a bit of personal experience. I suggest you don't listen to me, or anyone else, and instead be your own authority and discover what works for you and your body. There have been a whole slew of movies and books on diet (*Eating Animals*, a book by Jonathan Safran Foer), on fast food (*Fast Food Nation*), on factory farming (*Food Inc.*), on the meat industry (*Forks Over Knives*), on our heavy reliance on corn (*King Corn*), and on the sugar-laced products in the middle aisles of grocery stores (*Fed Up*). Do your research. Make up your own mind.

I have found that a high protein, high green vegetable diet works for me. I enjoy meat, and don't expect to give it up anytime soon. My oldest daughter has been a vegetarian for 10 years and is quite happy with her decision. On my diet, I feel full of energy, I can work out hard 5 days a week, I allow myself one day a week in which I can eat anything I want, all of which feels very supportive. What works for you? Find out what you are putting in your body, and then make an educated choice about what you will continue to put in your body.

Another thing I found to be incredibly supportive of my physical body is to drink more water, and less caffeine.

Here are a few good reasons to drink more water:

Drinking water helps maintain the balance of body fluids.

Water can help control calories.

Water helps energize muscles.

Water helps keep skin looking good.

Water helps your kidneys.

Water helps maintain normal bowel function.

Since my body is over 60% water, it just makes sense to me to remain well hydrated. I see a gas tank that I keep topping off. I don't go crazy about it, and drink so much water that I have to go to the bathroom every hour, but I will choose water over a soft drink when I go to a restaurant. I will carry a big bottle of water with me so I have it readily available. Again, this is what works for me. What works for you?

Regarding the frequency and nature of an exercise routine, I find that 5 days a week works for me. I need those two off days, usually the weekend, to rest and recover. I am not so concerned about building muscle, so I focus on 3 days of strong aerobic exercise. The other 2 days I do 30 minutes of weight lifting. Each workout includes stretching, and a hot sauna or steam room. I actually like to meditate in the hot steam, and it is the last thing I do before hitting the shower. It is one of my favorite parts of the workout, and serves as a reward for my hard work in the gym. I have also learned to be flexible with my routine. As I write this, I am sitting in the Coffee Lab in Phuket, Thailand. There is not a health club conveniently located near my home, so instead of aerobic machines and weights, I walk a 4-mile route to Surin Beach and back. At the beach, I swim for half an hour, which trains my abs and upper body. Go with the flow. Can you commit to working out on a regular schedule? What type of workout can you get behind and stick to? What will work for you?

Here is another thing that will greatly impact your physical body. It is my observation that most of the world does not know how to properly breathe. This is dumbfounding. We can live without food for weeks at a time and survive. We can live without water for days at a time and survive. Air, however, we can only go a few minutes before we expire. We need to breathe to live. Breath is life. And no one has ever spoken up and said, "This is the best way to breathe."

I discovered the importance of air and the ability to breathe on a trip to Maui 15 years ago. I was snorkeling in 15 feet of water. Down at the bottom of the water was an arch of coral. It looked like there was 2-3 feet of clearance, and for some reason that still belies any logic, I decided to take a deep breath, and descend 15 feet to swim through the arch. I got about half way through, and then my body was stuck. The clearance was not as big as I had estimated, and my body would not fit through the opening. I found myself pinned under the arch, now completely terrified, panicked, with images of my life racing through my head (this really does happen). This was, and still is, the most scared I have ever been.

So there I was, 15 feet under the water, stuck under a piece of choral, with all the air I needed just 15 feet above my head. My instincts took over, my will to live kicked in hard, and I grabbed both sides of the choral, and pushed myself through the opening, scratching up my waist on both sides, but getting through and rising toward the surface. I slowly swam to the shore, and got out of the water, well aware that I had just cheated death. My ability to do "stupid shit" has dramatically diminished since that incident.

There are plenty of resources on how to achieve a deep full breath. I have listed a few good exercises below. It is important that we become aware of our breath, and notice when we are reverting to shallow breathing, so we can resume deep full breaths. Most people don't even realize how they take short, shallow breaths. The impact of a fast shallow breathing (hyperventilating) is rather profound. Studies are showing that this type of breathing is putting too much air in your system, and this leads to both illness and chronic diseases.

This physiological condition (shallow breathing) is the main reason why people need to breathe a higher quantity of air. In 1988, physiologists researching at Duke University discovered that "the brain, by regulating breathing, controls its own excitability." This research indicates that poor breathing is the primary cause of delusions, mood swings, phobias, and other mental illnesses.

In other words, when someone breathes shallowly, their blood vessels constrict and cannot transport oxygen to the brain in any efficient manner. As a result, the brain becomes "excitable" and starts to activate random neural pathways. In the late 1960s and 1970s, a Russian doctor, Dr. Buteyko, discovered that efficient, proper breathing can cure over 200 chronic diseases, including obesity, and some cases of mental illness.

Here are two exercises you can do during meditation to develop the practice of full deep breaths. Once you have settled in for your meditation, place your hand over your belly button. Start consciously breathing into your belly so that your hand rises and falls to a relatively significant degree with each breath. Continue breathing this way for 100 deep breaths, counting each full breath (inhale and exhale) as one number. You may get distracted and forget which number you were on throughout the exercise. When that happens, just notice and start again. Always return to your breath, and notice the depth of your breath.

I learned this second exercise from a 30 day Tony Robbins program I listened to back in the '90s. The goal of this exercise is to breathe with a ratio of a 1 second inhale, 4 second hold, and 2 second exhale. Ideally, you will be able to inhale for 7 seconds, hold for 28, and exhale for 14. If you can only start with 3-12-6, that's ok. Start wherever you are and keep building up until 7-28-4 becomes natural.

Perform this cycle (inhale-hold-exhale) 10 times.

The best part of this whole process is that once you start breathing correctly, you have an entire system of preventative and counteractive medicine permanently located within your body. And it's all free! You will gradually find yourself experiencing higher levels of baseline happiness and shorter periods of sadness when they occasionally occur. Think about it: no one breathing in a relaxed, deep manner is stressed out. Similarly, you can't engage in fight-or-flight responses when breathing from your stomach. When this type of deep breathing becomes your natural, default way to take in oxygen, your entire body will run more efficiently and your energy levels/happiness will skyrocket!

Now that we have the breathing under control, let's tackle the next elephant in the room, sleeping. I can't tell you how many of my friends don't even remember that last time they had a solid, uninterrupted 8 hours of sleep. Job pressure, work deadlines, finances, relationship concerns, going to the bathroom, bad habits and an unsupportive environment all contribute to poor sleep. I remember reading my first Robert Ludlum novel on vacation in Cabo San Lucas. It was called *The Aquitaine Progression*, and the main character, Joel Converse, a typical superspy badass, kept making the statement, "Sleep is a weapon." As I started to study sleep, I soon realized that by just adding 2 hours of sleep to my typical 6 hours, I would be able to function at a much higher level. Why?

Sleep deficiency dumbs you down. Sleep plays a critical role in thinking and learning. Lack of sleep hurts these cognitive processes in many ways. First, it impairs attention, alertness, concentration, reasoning, and problem solving. This makes it more difficult to learn efficiently. Second, during the night, various sleep cycles play a role in "consolidating" memories in the mind. If you don't get enough sleep, you won't be able to remember what you learned and experienced during the day. Sleep disorders and chronic sleep loss can put you at risk for heart disease, heart attack, heart failure, irregular heartbeat, high blood pressure, stroke and diabetes.

Sleep deficiency also kills your sex drive. That's not good! Sleep specialists say that sleep-deprived men and women report lower libidos and less interest in sex. Depleted energy, sleepiness, and increased tension may be largely to blame. For men with sleep apnea, a respiratory problem that interrupts sleep, there may be another factor in the sexual slump. A study published in the *Journal of Clinical Endocrinology & Metabolism* in 2002 suggests that many men with sleep apnea also have low testosterone levels. In the study, nearly half of the men who suffered from severe sleep apnea also secreted abnormally low levels of testosterone during the night.

Over time, lack of sleep and sleep disorders can also contribute to the symptoms of depression. In a 2005 Sleep in America poll, people who were diagnosed with depression or anxiety were more likely to sleep fewer than six hours at night. The most common sleep disorder, insomnia, has the strongest link to depression. In a 2007 study of 10,000 people, those with insomnia were five times as likely to develop depression as those without. In fact, insomnia is often one of the first symptoms of depression. Insomnia and depression feed on each other. Sleep loss often aggravates the symptoms of depression and depression can make it more difficult to fall asleep. On the positive side, treating sleep problems can help depression and its symptoms, and vice versa.

Not getting enough sleep also makes you look older. Most people have experienced sallow skin and puffy eyes after a few nights of missed sleep. But it turns out that chronic sleep loss can lead to lackluster skin, fine lines, and dark circles under the eyes. When you don't get enough sleep, your body releases more of the stress hormone cortisol. In excess amounts, cortisol can break down skin collagen, the protein that keeps skin smooth and elastic. Sleep loss also causes the body to release too little human growth hormone. When we're young, human growth hormone promotes growth. As we age, it helps increase muscle mass, thicken skin, and strengthen bones

Sleep deficiency also makes you forgetful. As I got into my 40s, I noticed on occasion I would walk into a room, and then forget why I had entered the room. Or I would have a great idea, and then go to the computer, and the idea was gone. This is actually what caused me to explore my memory loss, and then discover what I could do to help get my memory back to its full functioning capacity. Are you trying to keep your memory sharp? Get plenty of sleep.

Not getting enough sleep also contributes to weight gain. When it comes to body weight, it may be that if you snooze, you lose. Lack of sleep seems to be related to an increase in hunger and appetite, and possibly to obesity. According to a 2004 study, people who sleep less than six hours a day were almost 30 percent more likely to become obese than those who slept seven to nine hours.

Recent research has focused on the link between sleep and the peptides that regulate appetite. Ghrelin stimulates hunger and leptin signals satiety to the brain and suppresses appetite. Shortened sleep time is associated with decreases in leptin and elevations in ghrelin. Not only does sleep loss appear to stimulate appetite, it also stimulates cravings for high-fat, high-carbohydrate foods. Ongoing studies are considering whether adequate sleep should be a standard part of weight loss programs.

Lack of sleep can affect our interpretation of events. This hurts our ability to make sound judgments because we may not assess situations accurately and act on them wisely. Sleep-deprived people seem to be especially prone to poor judgment when it comes to assessing what lack of sleep is doing to them. In our increasingly fast-paced world, functioning on less sleep has become a kind of badge of honor. But sleep specialists say if you think you're doing fine on less sleep, you're probably wrong. And if you work in a profession where it's important to be able to judge your level of functioning, this can be a big problem.

Studies show that over time people who are getting six hours of sleep, instead of seven or eight, begin to feel they've adapted to that sleep deprivation – they've gotten used to it. But if you look at how they actually do on tests of mental alertness and performance, they continue to go downhill. There's a point in sleep deprivation when we lose touch with how impaired we are.

Here are some suggestions to help with getting 8 hours of sleep. First, you have to commit. It is not as easy as you might think. My body was used to getting 6 hours. I was prideful about my ability to function on 5-6 hours. Commit so that when you don't get immediate results, you will stay the course.

1. Don't eat right before you go to bed.

2. Before going to bed, allow at least 15 minutes to decompress from the day.

3. Just before going to bed, replay the activities of your day, in reverse order, in your mind. This really works for me. Somehow it kind of unwinds my day, and allows me to let go of any discordant thoughts from the day.

   It would go something like this...

   "I got into bed. Before that, I did some work on my computer. Before that, I talked to my daughter. Before that, I had dinner. Before that, I drove home from work. During work, I saw 4 clients. I also talked to my boss. Before work, I ate a good breakfast."

4. Consume peaceful content. For example, read good fiction. This seems to take the mind off of all of your concerns, and immerses you in a good story. Or listen to some peaceful music. I have some ocean sounds, bird sounds, meadow sounds, rain sounds (my favorite), all of which allow me to calm my mind.

5. Make your room a black out room. Do what you have to do to make your room devoid of light. With all our high tech items, there are many sources of LED light. I have several pieces of cloth I use to cover up the sources of light. Or I turn everything off for

the night. I used to have my Iphone charging all night, which was not good for the phone. Now I charge before going to bed, and unplug it overnight. It's best, if possible, to remove all electronics from your bedroom all together. I can't do that, but I do turn most everything off, or cover it with a dark scarf. I also use eye pads to cover my eyes, and earplugs to keep things quiet.

Assignment:

1. Evaluate your diet. Make any changes that will support your health.

2. Work out once in the next 24 hours. Even if that means taking a short walk.

3. Take a few deep breaths and notice how good it feels. Try one of the breathing exercises.

4. Good night, dear reader. 8 hours. Commit. Take the necessary action. I will meet you on the other side.

Step 20

Purification

"Solitude is the place of purification."

—Martin Buber

Purification is the process of returning something back to its pure essence. For example, many years ago I undertook a 28-day cleanse. During those 28 days, I only ate fruits and vegetables. I took a few supplements that were recommended to remove toxins from my system. Over the 28 days, I lost 30 pounds, endured several enemas and concluded day 28 with a colonic irrigation. The purpose of this purification process was to return me to optimal health. By removing all the extra weight and gunk from my system, I moved closer to my pure and natural physical state.

I do recommend cleanses and fasts from time to time, mostly to put my ego in its place and shut the little bastard up for a while. The ego does not like change, and does not like to go without. But once convinced that I mean business, all gets slow and quiet, and that is a very welcome respite from my ego's constant bantering. The same is true with meditation. At first, the ego has quite a bit to say, all in an attempt to dissuade you from your quiet time. But after a few minutes, and nothing has changed, it does get quiet and inner realms are revealed.

However, the purification I am referring to in this step is the ongoing purification of your energy body and your spirit. There are people out there, which I will refer to as energy vampires, who will suck the life right out of you. You know who they are. Being around them is a drag. Being around an energy vampire requires so much work, and the experience is so unsatisfying. And in the end, you endured their presence and gave away your precious energy, which could have been used for far more deserving purposes.

I have meditated quite a bit in my life. There is a quiet place of peace, which I feel during each meditation session. If you have done meditation, you know what I am referring to. And with practice, during any time of the day, you can close your eyes and return to that centered place. Think of that place as home, and the process of purification requires that I manage my life so as to stay as close to that quiet center as possible.

Life and my ego have a way of throwing up roadblocks to my quiet center. Not only does life throw energy vampires my way, but there are all kinds of negative feelings and emotions that are randomly generated. It is not hard to rage against the machine. Most of us are living in a system that provides very little positive news. Deaths, murders, illnesses, accidents, tsunamis and hurricanes all crescendo on the non-stop 24 hour news channels. How can we not be impacted by all this negativity? We are, and it is our job to limit the damage, take a deep breath, and return to center.

Truly, purification is a process of understanding and dealing with the ego. Of course, there are external circumstances that can tip us this way or that. But it is how we respond to this external stimulus that determines just how pure and pristine we can maintain our energy. Your energy is one of the most valuable commodities you have. You are the caretaker of your own internal vibration. Cherish it. Reward it. Guard it. It is all you've got.

Assignment:

Identify an energy vampire in your life. Commit to spend as little time as possible with that person. Identify someone who has the type of life and energy you aspire to have. Make an effort to become more involved in that person's life. It is time for an upgrade.

Step 21

Technology Hiatus

"There is a loneliness in this world so great that you can see it in the slow movement of the hands of a clock."
— Charles Bukowski

We have an overabundance of stimuli. We all carry around some type of phone, be it a standard cell phone or a smart phone. They ring, they beep, the buzz, they vibrate, and they demand our attention many times throughout the day. Now we also have tablets, thin and light laptops, smart watches, and even glasses that work to interpret our experiences. It is a bit much. This step suggests that we might all be better off if we managed our technology better, spent less time online, and spent more time away from the television.

Idea #1 – Schedule technology-free time zones. For example, when you wake up, spend your first two hours without any technology. Don't check your email. Don't check Facebook. Don't post your newest photos. Think about how much good work you can get done with 2 uninterrupted hours. This idea takes control from the technology and puts it back in your hands.

Idea #2 – Reduce to five the number of email lists to which you are subscribed. I used to get over 100 emails a day that had absolutely no meaning to me. I would spend 10-15 minutes just deleting all the crap. I committed to reduce my list to five. It took over 2 weeks to get to the point where I only received 5 emails. Some of these lists are resistant to dropping you. Stick with it. Can you imagine only getting 5 emails from lists, and all the rest are from legitimate friends and family? Get to it.

Idea #3 – No phones at mealtime. I instituted this rule with my daughter. We muted our phones and placed them face down on the table. We actually talked to each other. It seemed foreign at first. We agreed that if either of us looked at our phone, that person would have to pay for the meal. It's pretty great. Conversation is becoming a lost art, but it does not have to be.

Recently I returned from the country of Laos. I had to leave Thailand in order to get a new Thai visa, and then return. My time in Thailand had passed by rather quickly. In fact, I can hardly believe I had already been there 3 months. The prospect of staying another 6 months just didn't seem all that long. I am very well aware of how magical my time in Thailand had been. I valued each day as if it could be my last. And so, the time did seem to fly by like a bullet whizzing past my French nose.

That week in preparation for my border run, I booked a ticket on Nok Airlines round trip to Udon Thani, a Thai city near the Laos border. I booked 3 nights at a hotel in Vientiane, Laos where the Thailand visa office is located. I took plenty of money and headed off into the wild blue yonder. It was all a bit last minute. It wasn't until I was in a mini van heading towards the Friendship Bridge, which connects Thailand to Laos, that I realized I had no idea if my life partner, my IPhone 5, would work in Laos. I do take my phone virtually everywhere I go. I do frequently set it on airplane mode so that I have plenty of me time. It is always there; ready to make a call, ready to post a photo, ready to slap a witty or observant thought on Facebook, or Skype an image to anyone of my children.

The Thailand phone service I have, AIS, did not work in Laos. I had no Internet connection! Lawdy, what to do? When I left the hotel and it's WIFI, I was like an untethered helium balloon barreling into space. At first, out of habit, I did go to my phone to post a picture to Instagram and was immediately reminded of my dire situation. I did not have an Internet connection. I went to Google maps to show a tuk tuk driver how to get back to my hotel. The app reminded me that I did not have an Internet connection. Then I had a breakthrough.

I was eating lunch on my second day with a friend. We had selected an Italian restaurant called Lao Luna. I had brought my phone, although in truth, it was only good to me as a camera. After two days, I had stopped going to it. I stopped the impulse. And then grace descended on me and time stood still. Until this moment, the trip to Laos was a bit of an inconvenience. The back and forth to the visa office, the problems that the slow hotel internet was causing me with my work, and having to adjust to a new currency and language all contributed to my Laos malaise. Then, it all shifted. Laos became beautiful. I was free. I felt like a kid in an Apple store (I feel certain more kids would prefer anything Apple makes to some candy!). I was playing old time hookey.

The food at that lunch was superb. I had a sea bass in a cream mushroom sauce, with a few potatoes and vegetables. The fish was excellently prepared. The weather was a perfect 72 (this is the temperature at which I do not notice the weather.) I experienced homeostasis with my environment. The sun was shining. People were smiling and happy, eating and talking and sharing life experiences, and I was embracing a new level of technology independence. It was a glorious transcendental moment in time.

As I write this, my IPhone 5 rests on the bed next to me. He seems to know that our relationship is going through a transition. He is back in Thailand, back online, fully charged, all topped up, and still he feels the distance between us growing. "I am sorry Jay's Iphone5 (his legal name), but I am going to be taking more me time. I hope that while I am out, and you are here at home guarding the castle, that you learn new ways to amuse yourself. You too can learn to be more independent. You don't need me in your life 24/7. This may be a bit painful at first, but it is the best thing for both of us. You stay here now. I am going outside to feel the sunshine on my face, free from any technological disturbance. Good bye buddy."

Idea #4 – Reduce the amount of time you spend watching television. This is by far the most important and valuable of the ideas (although they are all so supportive of you and your energy body). I have found that when I watch television, my spirit gets jarred in so many ways.

First of all, a television screen blinks at 30 times per second. Consciously, we may not notice it. But subconsciously we do notice it and feel it. Tests were conducted on children, and after watching television; they behave in a more agitated manner.

The content of television also creates stress. The commercials alone work brilliantly to create a demand for a myriad of products. In each hour, there are some 20 commercials, all created by experts in the fine art of desire creation. It is a huge energy drain to be in a constant state of want. How exhausting!

Studies in both children and adults have found an association between the number of hours of television watched and obesity. A study found that watching television decreases the metabolic rate in children to below that found in children at rest. TV watching and other sedentary activities are associated with greater risk of heart attack.

Let me state that I'm not saying television in its entirety is bad for you. There are times when it's nice to kick back and watch the game with your friends. This idea is more geared toward those who spend an abnormal amount of time in front of the tube on a daily basis. You know exactly who you are. I know there are countless studies on how television is bad for you, but here are some of the harmful effects I see that most studies don't cover when it comes to watching too much TV.

The biggest trap of watching too much TV is that it becomes a safe way to escape your own life instead of looking at it square in the eye. If you find yourself watching hours of television everyday, it might be good to think about whether or not it's a subtle indication to yourself that your life is not what you want it to be, that it's not interesting enough so you feel the need to immerse yourself in the lives of others.

People who gossip have the same problem. Their lives aren't interesting, so they feel the need to know everybody else's business and spread the word to whoever will listen. The person who watches television for hours on end is no different. They end up so wrapped up in the lives of others that it becomes their entire life.

When you watch TV, you'll find that it does all the work for you. You don't need to "create" in your mind like you do when reading. When you read, your brain has to use its imagination to come up with the smells, the tastes, the sounds, the pictures, and the feelings described in the book or article, but when you watch TV, all of that is already done for you (at least the hearing and seeing part). If you ever wonder why your brain feels so "empty" after watching television, that's exactly why. Your brain shuts off because it has no job to do. Use it or lose it indeed.

People literally "sleep through life" by watching hours of television a day. It's a tragedy that they cannot see the time they spend there can be used to better their own life, so they don't have to feel the need to escape it. Along the lines of that, have you ever tried to get things done after watching TV? It's as if you've become "mind paralyzed" and you have to wait for your brain to slowly get back in gear. I call that time period the "dead zone," and even after that, you're still not working at peak efficiency.

This is the worst part of watching too much television. TV can be just as addictive as any illegal substance on the market today. It's easily accessible, pleasurable, and makes you forget your troubles for the day. Sound familiar? You watch one show and when it ends, the TV says "Coming up next...stay tuned for blah blah blah," so you become curious, you watch it and you like it and BOOM, you add another rotation to your weekly TV schedule. Those hours add up and once you get vested in the shows, they've got you for life.

Watching television for hours on end is the easy way out and many people choose to take it. Why? Because watching television for hours a day switches off our brains so we don't have to think about our own lives. When it's time to turn the TV off and reality comes to bite us in the rear, what do the majority of us do then? We retreat into the safe confines of television once again.

TV can easily become the biggest time thief of all, and yet, people don't realize it. They don't become indignant at the opportunities in life that they lose. It's amazing how people take the time to buy the best security for their home so their precious belongings don't get stolen, but when it comes to protecting their mind and their time, two of their biggest assets, the doors are wide open for easy pickings. People have got to realize that the quality of their lives can become so much better if they just take the time to stop watching TV and channel that energy toward creating the life they want to live.

Here's a thought. Unplug the box and put it high up in your closet so it's a pain in the butt to reach. You'll learn to live without it. The sun will shine that much brighter, food will taste that much better, and life will be that much sweeter.

Just the other day, I sat down for breakfast at a little restaurant on Loi Kroh Road, Crema Café in Chiang Mai. While I had spent the last 2 months in Phuket, my breakfast was primarily chicken and iced coffee. My go to spot was a hole in the wall that served chicken in different curries and soups. Arriving in Chiang Mai, and living in a more touristy section of downtown, I have more food choices. I can eat a hamburger, a burrito, a mango smoothie, and a wide swath of Thai delicacies (including stewed pork leg). On this day, I ordered a cheese omelet, which came with a piece of toast. There, next to the toast was a small package of butter, the kind that you might see at

Denny's.

Shock and distress coursed through my veins. Butter. It had been 2 months not only since I ate butter, but also since I had even seen butter. You must understand, I am the guy who frequently states with great glee, "Butter makes everything better!" My children have looked at me with disgust when I put butter on the crust of my pizza. Egads. While in England, I discovered a butter called Lurpak. The local bakery made bread on Monday. I would go to the store in the morning, buy the bread (often still warm), cut a nice slice, toast it, and then slather on the Lurpak. I can say with absolute certainty that there was no happier nor content human being on the planet save for me at the moment the toasted Lurpak coated bread hit my palate.

So how did I break the habit? How is it that I did not eat butter for 2 months? I moved to Thailand. How is it that I no longer sit in front of a television and waste hours of my life surfing from channel to channel? I moved to Thailand. While I don't' expect many people to move to Thailand for the winter, there are two valuable lessons we can glean from this experience. First, take on a big project so that you don't' have the time nor inclination to eat crap and watch tv. Second, remove the vices out of sight. Get them out of the house. If you don't see a TV or butter, you are less likely to use them. If you want to quit smoking, the first thing you do is get rid of the cigarettes, and clean out all ashtrays and anything else that may remind you of smoking. I quit smoking over four years ago.

I saw a post on Facebook. "Mother Theresa didn't walk around complaining about her thighs. She had shit to do." If I am focusing on my work and my health, I don't have time to vegetate in front of the TV. What can you commit to that will propel you to a place where TV doesn't make sense? Are there any foods in your home that you know aren't healthy, that you can throw out or give to someone? The answer to these questions may be No. You may love your TV time and relish the idea of gorging on pizza and butter. I have been there too, and I had a pretty good time... for a while. Eventually, my spirit had enough, and demanded something deeper from me, something that require my full presence. Butter and TV make me sleepy. For me, it was time to wake up.

When it's all said and done, watching too much television provides you with a safe escape from looking at your own life, deteriorates your mind, makes you unproductive, and can lead to a dangerous addiction. It truly is one of the most dangerous drugs out there on the market today and the sad thing is that most people don't even realize it. This step invites you to engage technology on your terms, in ways that will be more supportive of you and the realization of your dreams.

Assignment:

Try out the ideas presented in this step. See how it feels. Pick one day and do not watch any television. See how that feels. If you feel like really going for it, don't watch any more TV for the rest of the week. Notice how much extra time you have, and how much more you can get done toward achieving your dreams.

Step 22

Nature Knows

"Climb the mountains and get their good tidings. Nature's peace will flow into you as sunshine flows into trees. The winds will blow their own freshness into you, and the storms their energy, while cares will drop away from you like the leaves of Autumn."
— John Muir

I don't know where you live. Nature may be just outside your back door. Or, you may have to drive a bit to get to nature. We are a part of nature, and I find for myself, I forget that fact and often feel disconnected from nature. When I return to nature, my heart breathes, and my sense of unity with all things returns. My favorite place to go is the ocean. I have had profound experiences at the ocean. One of my favorite pastimes is to go to the ocean with some new music loaded on my IPhone, sit in a meditative pose on the beach, and look and listen. Pure heaven.

There are no straight lines in nature. Have you ever noticed that? Everything is round, or wavy, or jumbled, or bendy. Even the long palm fronds outside my house grow straight but bend over time. Nature is a beautiful metaphor for life. We would like to believe there are straight lines for us to follow. But there aren't. You may structure your life to head in one direction toward your vision, but you won't be able to get there by going along a straight line. Life is messy. Life has it's own path for you, and it is not straight.

As a kid, we use to play with walnut shells. My brothers and I had a ditch that ran along the street in front of our house. When it rained, water would stream through the ditch. This was pure ecstasy for 8-year-old Jay and my motley crew of friends. We would make damns, destroy dams, make side eddies, and best of all, race walnut shells. We would imagine we were inside those walnut shells, shooting the rapids of our ditch. No matter what we did, those walnut shells would float from one end of the ditch to the other end of the ditch. But each time, the path would be slightly different. The water might flow this way or that way at any given time. Sometimes there were rocks in the way, and the walnuts would work their way around the rocks, always moving toward the final destination downstream.

Do you see the metaphor? This is life. We may feel like we are in the walnut shell controlling our path, but ultimately, we are all heading in the direction of our path. Nature teaches me that it is ok to take my hands off the tiller of my boat of life. There really is no need to try to control everything because a) I can't, and b) it truly doesn't make much if any difference in determining where I am going. Best of all, hands off the tiller is far more enjoyable, more magical, and more adventurous. In the end, it leaves one with a life well lived.

Recently, I ventured out of the city of Chiang Mai, Thailand and into the countryside. I rode an elephant, visited a rural village filled with children, scarves, pigs and chickens and surrounded by pastoral rice fields. We hiked a ways from the village to a secluded waterfall throwing off mist and rainbows in the air. After lunch we headed out for our final activity, which was bamboo rafting down a fast moving river.

There were four of us, a wonderful German family of three and the lone American, who boarded our ship. Our captain was a young Thai man, early twenties, who with the use of a large stick guided us around rocks and fellow rafters. Once we boarded the raft, we sat down. The shock of the cold water on our behinds was immediate. As we pulled away from the shore, more water filled my swimsuit, creating another shock to the system. I noticed everyone had pulled their legs up, so that only their behinds and feet could get wet. I instinctively knew to drop my legs and let everything get wet as quickly as possible. I knew to surrender to the cold, for certainly more was coming my way.

As we moseyed down the river, the rapids got bigger, and larger waves of water enveloped us. After about 5 minutes, my legs had adjusted to the temperature and the water started to feel warm. Suddenly everything shifted. The rafting portion of our adventure had become a glorious dive into oneness, a transformation from cold and unknown to warmth and communion. I had experienced this before, so I had an idea of what to expect.

There I was, a floating orb of light, feeling the warmth of a late afternoon as I was effortlessly carried down river. The raft was a womb and I was the perfectly vulnerable and ecstatic passenger. The sunlight danced in and out through the trees, while butterflies of all colors mingled in and out of my Technicolor dream. Sometimes, and this may happen to you as well, I have the experience of being exactly where I am suppose to be, and everything, absolutely everything, is perfect and in no need of a change or fix.

At one point, the German mother asked the father, "this is nice, isn't it?" to which the father begrudgingly said "it's all right." I heard his response and realized in that moment the profound impact that our perception has on the quality of our experiences in life. In the most general terms, the more perceptive you are, the more you will experience and the more coherent will be your own philosophy of life. In this case, if I were living in a place of constant judgment of my experiences, I would have robbed myself of the transcendental journey I had the privilege to experience.

Certainly I would assert that as one increases his or her powers of perception, there is a logical understanding of the value of letting go rather than clenching and holding tight. Increased perception lead to an opening to life. It is for this reason that many of my weekend events focus on processes to aid in increasing perception, and stretch our understanding of different realms of reality. It is my observation that there are few things more exuberant than realizing you are now perceiving the world in a new and previously unrealized way. It is like walking out of a darkened room into the sunlight.

Take me to the river. Experience the magic of nature. During that raft ride, colors were popping. Butterflies were flirting with me. The water had a conversation with me. I flew through the trees, and saw me back on the raft. Everyone on the shore smiled at me like they were all in on it. It's like that. Call it the zone. Call it Samadhi. Call it connecting with nature. Call it returning home. For me, it was experiencing my true nature with and not apart from anything. Thank you Thailand for your wonderful and mystical land. It has been an honor to walk your soil and float on your water. All of this and more is readily available in nature.

The invitation of this step is to put your cell phone someplace safe at home, remove your watch, and then go to a place in nature. Take a walk, sit down at the beach, find a little spot of grass at a park, and breathe it all in. Ask nature to give you a message, and then listen. You may be amazed at what you can learn by sitting attentively in nature. Ask for guidance with a question or problem you are dealing with, and then see what nature has to say. Feel the wind, observe the clouds, listen for birdcalls, and see what is happening at your feet with our insect friends. Take in as much as you can, and allow nature to speak to you. Nature will tell you the truth. Train you heart to hear it.

Assignment:

Spend 1 hour of quality alone time in nature. At the end of the time, write down how you felt after having spent the time in nature.

Step 23

Drugs, Medicine and Sacred Ritual

"Nature loves courage. You make the commitment and nature will respond to that commitment by removing impossible obstacles. Dream the impossible dream and the world will not grind you under, it will lift you up. This is the trick. This is what all these teachers and philosophers who really counted, who really touched the alchemical gold, this is what they understood. This is the shamanic dance in the waterfall. This is how magic is done. By hurling yourself into the abyss and discovering its a feather bed."

— Terence McKenna

What role, if any, do drugs have in raising one's consciousness? Can drugs help us to achieve radical freedom? Are drugs essential, or are they rather a curiosity to explore if and when you have the inclination and time to do so? In this step, I will share a few experiences I have had over the years. I took these various drugs to learn more about me, about the world, about other dimensions, and ultimately, about the transformation of man.

Like most American college students, I tried the usual suspects of legal and illegal drugs, alcohol, marijuana and cocaine. At that point in my life, taking drugs was more of a social experience, a way to loosen the boundaries between me and others, a method to connect in ways that weren't readily available without the effects of the drugs. After college, and well into my forties, I was an occasional drinker and cigarette smoker, and that was about it. It wasn't until I reached my forties, and my passion for self-discovery had fully bloomed, that I began to explore the outer realms with ecstasy, mushrooms, ayahuasca and DMT.

It was 1999 when I had my first experience with ecstasy. Ecstasy is a drug that comes in many different formulations, often combining the primary drug of MDMA with caffeine, methamphetamine and/or ephedrine, all of which have similar stimulant effects to MDMA. You can also take pure MDMA raw (awful tasting stuff) or in capsule form. There are websites you can visit to determine the pill you will be taking, which often has an identifying color and stamp, to show the mix of ingredients. In any case, buyer beware, as any yahoo can start pressing pills, using any color and stamp, and then selling for a profit. Ideally, you trust your source, which has already tried and can verify the safety and efficacy of the pill.

I was in Australia with a group of about 20 people. We were staying in a large house. We were 5 days into a 7-day workshop when we were informed about the opportunity to try ecstasy. I had never tried the drug, had not really heard much about it, but was keen to give it a go. I like the name of it. Over the next 5 years, I would estimate that I used ecstasy about 20 times. I haven't used it at all in the past 10 years. Ecstasy is definitely one of my favorite drug experiences. I remember my first experience, feeling my heart expand as waves of serotonin flooded my brain. It is a glorious feeling. I remember asking myself how I had never felt this before? I also noticed that my thought process became very clear, and fast. Ideas kept popping into my head. I remember spending an hour or two with a friend, who has also taken the ecstasy, and as we spoke, we kept getting off on these wonderful tangents, then back to our main conversation, and then off again on a tangent, and on and on.

My biggest take away from ecstasy is that I had been living with a closed heart. Once I felt just how open my heart could be, I have found that openness available to me at any time, with ecstasy or without. My ecstasy experiences trained me how to be a heart warrior. I continued to feel how connected we all are, and how marvelous it is to be spiritually intimate with another. But again, the main point for me was that I could take this learning and apply it to my day-to-day life. For me, this makes ecstasy a tool, and not a crutch. It opened a door, and now I can walk through it and back at will.

Well, to use a school metaphor, if ecstasy is elementary school, ayahuasca is graduate school. That is how big the leap is in experiences. Ayahuasca is a powerful hallucinogen. This cannot be overstated. Aya, as it is called, is a combination of two plants that can be found in the Amazon jungle. These two plants are put in water, and cooked down until you are left with a most unctuous thick brown liquid. Truly, the taste of Aya is revolting. From the year 2000 to the year 2005, I participated in about a dozen ayahuasca rituals, in Australia, the USA, and in Peru.

Ayahuasca, lovingly referred to as Peruvian roulette, is serious medicine. This is not a "let's get high!" type of experience. Properly administered, an ayahuasca ceremony requires a skilled, trained and experienced shaman. It is the shaman who provides the ayahuasca, who holds space for the ritual, who arranges for the music, and who, most importantly, handles any issues that arise. I have been blessed to work with a few different shamans who were amazing in their ability to support a group of spiritual travelers through to the end of the journey. I will share about 5 different ayahuasca journeys, all of which happened in chronological order.

My very first journeys took place over one week in the rainforest in Australia. Five women and I were participating in 3 journeys over 5 days. For most of us, this would be our first experience with ayahuasca. My wife at the time had experienced the 5 day event just a few weeks before. She called me at the end of her experience and told me to get on a plane and get there. Three days later, I landed in Australia and was ready to go.

My very first journey was gentle and healing. I am grateful it was this way, as it propelled me forward, enthusiastic about more journeys. The reason ayahuasca is called Peruvian roulette is because one's experience can be very intense in one direction or the other. As you will read, I had one hellish journey. Had my first journey been intense and painful, I doubt I would have continued on the ayahuasca path. Instead, I was led by the hand by spirit guides, and lain down on a warm soft table. Once the journey begins, guides often lead me throughout the experience. It is remarkable really, for I am conscious, not high or drunk as you might feel on alcohol or marijuana, but instead feeling clear headed and able to interact with these beings that have appeared in my consciousness.

Once I had lain down on this table, more beings, flying beings, like hovering crystals, began to emit the 7 colors of the chakras (red, orange, yellow, green, blue, indigo, violet) on each of my chakras. I immediately began to weep, for I realized at a very deep cellular level, these beings with their light were healing me of my past hurts and painful experiences. I felt water streaming down the side of my head as I looked up from the ground. I don't know how long this went on, but it felt like a couple of hours. It remains the most healing experience of my life, and certainly the best cry, or release, I have had. At some point, the healing creatures left, their work complete. I opened my eyes, and saw the others in the circle. I heard the shaman playing his guitar, and slowly eased back into the room, hearing music as if for the first time. Cobwebs were replaced with clarity, and my body felt light and moved with a newfound ease.

The final Aya journey of that same week was much different than the first healing journey. I did not have the same dramatic visual light show experience. Instead I had a more visceral bodily response to the ayahuasca. I felt much more connected to the Earth, and to the creatures of the Earth, and particularly of the rainforest in which I found myself. I saw the bugs, and leeches, and birds, and experienced life from their point of view, which for me, was singularly to survive. I remember having a powerful experience of "live and let live." The highlight was at about 3 in the morning when I met a snake in the jungle. I knew of the significance of the serpent, and it was with great respect that I watched and observed his movements. I did not fear the serpent, but felt more of a teacher – student relationship.

Here's the thing. The serpent wanted to eat me. He was a very large snake, with a triangular face colored black and green, who carried a dignity about him. In the moment, I felt honored, unsure of how the process would feel, but open to whatever came next. The serpent approached and quickly opened his mouth and consumed me whole. It was dark for a while, and then I sort of dissolved and became one with the rainforest floor. I was the Earth from which the plants grew to life. It was a profound experience of the circle of life, and the sanctity of life for all beings. I also learned a lesson about acceptance, and my willingness to go with the flow, and to stop trying to control so many aspects of my life.

The next ayahuasca experience was some 4 years later, and took place in my hometown area of Sonoma County. I had heard about a shaman from Peru who was very gifted, and had been guiding Aya journeys for over 20 years. I really wanted to attend his 10-day event in Peru, which included doing 5 journeys over 10 days, eating a very restricted diet, and living in isolation except when participating in the rituals. In order to attend, I needed to attend a couple of local journeys as part of a vetting process. The 10-day dieta (diet) would be an intense experience, and certainly was not designed for those who were merely curious.

My first journey with the shaman took place on a Friday night. I was in a circle with about 20 people, most very experienced with ayahuasca, and my intention was to attend 2 rituals in a row, Friday and Saturday night. The first journey lives as the most prolonged bit of terror I have ever experienced. It all started, as all the rituals do, with each of us walking up to the shaman one by one, and then being handed a little shot glass full of the ayahuasca. You take your drink in a gulp, experience the horrid taste, give a little bow of acknowledgement to the shaman, and head back to your seat. Some shamans require the participants to stay upright, while others will allow you to lie down. He was an upright shaman, hardcore to the end.

I took my first drink, sat down, and waited. The effects of ayahuasca are not often immediately felt, say like the warm rush you might feel drinking a shot of tequila. You can begin to feel the initial effects in as short as 15 minutes and as long as an hour. Now I must say at this point in my story, that I let my ego get the best of me. I knew absolutely nothing about the strength of this shaman's brew. I only knew that after 30 minutes, I had not felt anything, so when offered a second drink, I stood up and had a second drink. Literally, within 5 minutes, I knew I had made a big mistake. I sweated with fear. I was slammed by a feeling of being on a fast moving train and it was only going to accelerate, and I had no way to get off the train, nor slow the train down. I was in for one hell of a ride for the next several hours, and I could not do anything about it.

I immediately stood up and insisted on leaving the circle and going outside. I wanted to get on the Earth, and attempt to feel grounded. I wanted to feel the air on my face, again to help bring me back from this runaway ayahuasca freight train I was straddling. These actions were like farts in the wind. I would have no choice but to ride this out, which I did. Fortunately, I did have the help of one of the shaman's assistants, who stayed close to me as I free fell into nothingness. What that looked like is this. I felt myself leave the planet. I was a spirit spiraling away from all I knew. I felt the loss of my family, and then the loss of humanity. I felt so alone, out there is deep dark space. Before long, I could not even remember who my family was, or what human beings were. I was losing all the ways I had come to identify myself as Jay.

I remember opening my eyes and looking at the woman who was with me, and imploring her to remind me that I would be coming back, that this experience would in fact end, and I could return to being a human being again. But then I was gone again, unable to resist the power of the ayahuasca. Soon I was unable to remember who I was. This was my death. The identity I had assumed of Jay was no longer. I could not remember anything. I was truly living in the now, for I had no choice. As hard as I tried to say to myself, "I am Jay," it meant nothing.

Jay died during that ayahuasca session, and as I said, it was the most prolonged terror I have ever felt. At some point, the Aya slowly began to wear off. I was invited to return to the circle and take my place. I then fell back into an altered state, for even though the most intense part of the journey was over, I still had a couple of hours to experience. I remember seeing a light and opening my eyes, and there was the shaman, standing right in front of me, his smiling gaze and knowing glint in his eyes welcoming me back.

Well, after that hellish experience, you would think I would do just about anything to get out of attending the Saturday night ritual. I did feel shell-shocked. I spent Saturday morning sleeping, and then sat is a hot tub for about an hour. And as I looked back at my experience, I began to feel grateful for the lessons I learned from the "death of Jay." Who are we if not our identity? Who am I once I am stripped of all the ways I identify myself? That journey put me on a path with some real answers. So after a light salad, I headed back to the venue for the follow up journey, with one mantra running through my head: "Don't take a second drink!"

The fourth journey I will share about was a journey of bliss. After my death experience, the following journey was a welcome home by my spirit guides. As the ayahuasca started to kick in, I could feel a wave of warmth as I was gently ushered into an alternate reality. The goddess Durga often shows up, with her many arms welcoming me to her sacred world. My heart immediately opened up, and I was treated to sounds, sights, insights and spiritual generosity of the many guides I encountered that night. Several of the other journeyers sang songs or played a musical instrument. It was glorious. I have never heard the human voice sound so pleasing and heartwarming as when I have experienced ayahuasca. This journey left me well aware of the many different ways an ayahuasca journey could go, and put a respectable amount of fear and appreciation for the serious nature of the 10-day dieta I had committed to attend in Peru in a few months time.

The last journey to share took place in Peru. I arrived in Lima, met the group, took another flight to a smaller city, drove to the Amazon, took a 2 hour boat ride to our venue, ate our last meal before beginning the dieta, and then we were led to our palapas, which would serve as my home for the next 10 days. I had a waterfall for my shower, and blue morphos butterflies floating by as my pets. At first I read voraciously, but soon learned to just hang out and watch the world go by without too much activity. This journey I will share about was the last of the five journeys during the dieta, which unlike all the other journeys I had ever undertaken, was done during the day. There would be no hiding in the dark.

The journey kicked in almost instantaneously. I remember getting up to go to the bathroom, and seeing a butterfly. The butterfly looked like a living Christmas tree ornament, radiant and casting off a prism of colors. The strongest brew had been saved for our final gathering. This journey showed me again that I am not my identity. I was able to completely detach my spirit from my body and all other forms of self-identification. We were treated to a thunderstorm, which I must say, on the medicine, was stellar and spectacular. What was also significant about this journey was that I knew it would be my last. I felt a completion, a done-ness, and a lack of curiosity and desire for where any future journeys might lead. I was done, grateful and complete.

The final experience to share is the most intense of all my drug experiences. Smoking DMT is a short experience, and probably the most intense of experiences you can have. My DMT experience in Australia made a huge impact in my ongoing awakening. I had just completed a 6 hour or so ayahuasca journey. It was now about 4 in the morning. The Shaman asked if anyone still wanted to have the DMT experience. I raised my hand and we began. Just to back up a bit, I had heard about DMT from friends and my teacher at the time. They had told me that smoking DMT was like being shot out of this reality into the heart of the universe.

One shaman had told me that, for about 2 weeks, I wouldn't be able to think about much of anything else after the experience, other than the experience. That was how "full-on" the experience could be. And, having just completed the ayahuasca experience, this DMT experience would most likely be longer in duration because I still had the ayahuasca coursing through my veins. Instead of the standard 15-minute experience, this DMT experience would last 45 minutes.

And so, I jumped. With hands trembling, I held onto the pipe and took my first inhalation, held it for a few seconds and let it out. Then I took my second inhalation and held it for a few seconds and felt a wave overcome me. I grabbed one of the Shaman's hands as I fell back into my cushioned space and entered a new reality. Consciously, I remember that my body began to tremble, as if a massive orgasm had enveloped me. Then I entered a place of such beauty, I could only sigh with awe. I have read about others who have had the full-blown DMT experience. This place I entered is commonly referred to as the dome. All my senses were heightened. I could hear the others who were holding space. I could hear their breathing.

To describe with words this place I visited would not do it justice. Words so often fail, as much of what we experience is indescribable. Bright colors were whirling about. Thousands of eyes lined the dome. I felt in the presence of the Universal All. Never had I experienced anything so beautiful. I felt held like never before. I felt loved like I didn't even know what love was. My greatest orgasm was a tickle in my nose compared to the feelings I had during this experience. Overall, I felt overcome and awed by the power, the speed, the perfection and the certainty of this place.

As I began to come back to the present reality, I recall looking at my hands and commenting to myself about how small they seemed. I had just come from a place of such grandeur, such exquisite magnificence, that the re-entry back was quite emotional. Suffice it to say, it was painful to leave. And, at the same time, I burst out into an outrageous fit of laughter that lasted some 15 minutes. When I spoke, the first thing I said was, "We are all just beating off!" By that I meant, I had spent all of my life trying to figure everything out, trying to control things, trying to make things happen. After this experience, I learned the lesson of Let Go. I realized that the energies we don't see, the supreme intelligence we sometimes feel, the brilliance of this perfect world, is far too fast, far too powerful, far to supreme, to think that anything I do is of any real consequence. In other words, let go of the controls and just enjoy the ride.

The ride is bumpy. The less control you exert, the more bumpy the ride. There is always a choice. You can control, and live a life devoid of any real exploration and growth. It is a calm ride (not the most satisfying ride in the amusement park!). Or, you can embark on the most glorious of rides, full throttle, hands off the wheel, and let the universe do with you what it will.

Every moment, every experience, each is an opportunity to engage and discard your false self. Every moment is an opportunity to let the fire burn. Rather than hanging out with a fire extinguisher, ready to spray, you will be free to burn and learn and grow. We are all on the road to awakening. It is in our nature to expose the false and return to our selves. Bliss is not what we are after. We are after something far more powerful and satisfying and permanent, freedom from the confines of our limited minds. My various drug experiences certainly impact my worldview, my sensitivity to energy, my powers of perception and my willingness to let go of my need to try to control everything. This was all very positive. My life would not be the same and I would not be the same had I not walked through these various doorways. Are drugs a part of your journey? That is a question I must leave you to answer.

Assignment:

Simply reflect on your feelings about drugs. Have you had some powerful transformative experiences? Are drugs taboo in your life? Is that your choice, or is it a choice that was made for you? What role does alcohol, marijuana or tobacco play in your life? What is the most supportive relationship with drugs for you?

Step 24

Like Water

"In one drop of water are found all the secrets of all the oceans; in one aspect of You are found all the aspects of existence."

— Khalil Gibran

A question that has served me well is, "What would water do?" I have learned that it is my ego that has brought about the most pain in my life and in the life of those I hold dear. My male friends, during our weekend events, have come to refer to ego as "little bastard." And you have to give it up to the little bastard. He is smart, deceptive, cut throat, and unrelenting. You can look at it like this: Ego is fire, and your inner self, your inner knowing, your inner peace is water.

What would water do? In 1999, I was riding high on the success of my network marketing business. I was on track to earn about $500,000 that year. I was flying first class to events in Australia, all over the Caribbean and Mexico. I was the first speaker at a 3,000 person event. I was on fire. During one of our events, I paid over $10,000 for a week for a suite at a resort in Mexico. Upon arriving, we were told that we would have to take the suite on the first floor, as the second floor suite was already occupied. Little bastard no likey.

I still recall how upset I was by this bit of news. Didn't they know who I was! How dare they inconvenience me and my family! No matter what my protestations, we were going to be staying the week in the suite on the first floor. Now, remember how I said discontent leads to breakthrough and transformation. Here is another example. I settled down and we had our bags brought to the room. Right out the window of our suite was the water. Certainly the "ocean view" was delivered as promised.

Suddenly, I felt layers and layers of stress melt from my body. I started to ask myself these questions: "What would it be like not to feel the need to have the best this and the best that all the time?" "What would it be like to accept life's twists and turns without protestations?" "What if I flowed with life, rather than battling life?" What would water do? It was a transformation in my life like few others. I felt acceptance, at peace, at a place in which I could turn over the tiller of my life's boat and simply enjoy the ride.

From that point forward, I have always stayed in the perfect room in my hotel or resort. Since my expectations had been dropped, anything I was given was absolutely without fault. I don't need to be on the top floor to feel higher than everyone else. Oprah can have the best suite in the place. I am happy wherever the universe puts me. Now, of course, this is not a chapter on selecting hotel rooms. This is a seminal lesson about the illusion of self will, which the ego will continue to tell you is not an illusion. The ego would have you think you are all-powerful, and there is no invisible hand leading the way. Ego says all of life falls on your shoulders, and he is there to help you out.

What would water do? Everybody wants to go up. Water wants to go down. Water will accept the terrain, and blend in. It is content with the places people disdain. Praise and disdain are just two sides of the same coin. Why fight for one and discard the other? Why not allow the forces that are shaping us determine the vector of our lives? Ego will tell me he knows what is best for me. I have come to believe the universe knows best as long as I don't resist and choose to serve as an obedient son.

Obedience is the final and greatest task we will undertake. Water obeys. Water and gravity are a perfect metaphor. Water does not fight gravity and try to rise up. Water acknowledges gravity as a fundamental force and therefore moves accordingly. The universal law is also a fundamental force, and the choice is ours to respect it or give it no quarter.

Next time you are feeling the stress of life, ask yourself, "What would water do?" Each and every time I do, I feel a wave of peace in my energy body. Just the thought of water is relaxing and empowering. Try it out. You will get some resistance from the little bastard, but he is only doing his job. Thanks for sharing chap, but I think this time I am going to take the path of least resistance. It just makes sense!

Assignment:

Recall a time where you experienced stress because you needed something or somebody to be a certain way. How would it have turned out, both for you and for the situation, had you eased off and allowed things to happen more naturally?

Step 25

Our Friend Fear

"Come to the edge."
"We can't. We're afraid."
"Come to the edge."
"We can't. We will fall!"
"Come to the edge."
And they came.
And he pushed them.
And they flew.

—Guillaume Apollinaire

You can't be an eagle without leaving the nest. Each day is an invitation to be magnificent. Each moment is an opportunity to spread your wings, your glorious resplendent wings, and show the world what one individual can contribute. Each breath is an opportunity to say what everyone wants to say, but are either afraid or unwilling to take a stand.

This is the choice. This is the day. This is the moment. This is the breath. The fear you feel, that feeling deep within, down in your root, is a sign, a guidepost that tells you you're on a powerful path towards full self-expression. You are on a path toward being one of the few who surrenders to fear, and does what only you can do. You have a story. It is a unique story. We want to hear it. But you have to be generous and courageous and willing to share it.

This is it. Come to the edge, jump off the ledge, leap into the free fall of creation. You are powerful. Your story is profound. You have risen from the ashes. You are an inspiration. Don't hold on. Let go of your limiting beliefs and fly. Do it for us. Do it for yourself. Close your eyes tonight knowing you nurtured yourself by supporting others. Leave the nest as only you can do and fly. Don't think. Listen, feel and respond. This is your time. Celebrate with us the utter brilliance of you.

What does it take to be free? It takes a mature relationship with fear. Very little is accomplished in an environment of comfort. Many are familiar with the concept of the comfort zone. If you are not familiar with the comfort zone analogy, imagine a cloud one lives in called the comfort zone. In the comfort zone, you may feel secure, content, pleased with your past accomplishments, and nestled in with your family. Daily existence occurs in the comfort zone, but not much else. Real accomplishment, authentic growth, and profound transformation takes place outside the comfort zone. As you may surmise, life outside of the comfort zone is, well, uncomfortable. It feels like you are doing things you may not know and may not completely understand, and which may make you feel fearful. But many of us march forward in spite of all these unpleasant feelings, because this is how we learn, this is how we grow, and this is how we accomplish great things in our life.

Author David Deida, who wrote a fabulous book entitled *The Way of the Superior Man*, speaks about the importance of living just at your edge.

"By leaning just beyond your fear, you challenge your limits compassionately, without trying to escape the feeling of fear itself. You step beyond the solid ground of security with an open heart. You stand in the space of unknowingness, raw and awake."

—David Deida

Living just at your edge requires one to live with a healthy dose of fear. Fear is a friend we all must get to know, learn to accept, and in fact, are required to embrace. If you do not know fear, you do not know yourself. If you have never pushed yourself beyond your comfort zone, how can you expect anyone else to do the same? In life, in order to be successful, in order to be in a position of freedom, you will need to lead others. The only way to lead others is to lead by example. There is no other way.

Be friends with your fear. Learn how to breathe through it. Become so adept at fear management that when you feel it, you are enlivened, and now have access to a powerful energy you may harness to do some good not only in your life, but in the world. Learning to deal with fear, and turning fear into your friend, is a powerful component of your mental tool kit.

Fear is that feeling in the pit of our stomach that forces us to stop and reevaluate any given situation. Fear is a beautiful mechanism that can, when operating properly, warn us of potentially life threatening situations. Fear is the trigger for our most natural human response of "fight or flight." Fear is what happens before anything of real importance occurs in our life. Fear keeps us honest. How we respond to fear at every turn determines not only the direction our life will take, but also how we will feel about ourselves after we have chosen a direction.

What is fear? At its root, fear is a feeling. It is nothing more and nothing less. For me, the feeling of fear is a full body sensation, kind of like an alarm clock going off deep inside. I don't usually get nauseous, but the feeling can be very intense at times. For some, the physical sensations can be overwhelming, and medication is necessary to achieve a balance. The point is that fear is a physical sensation. How we react to these physical sensations is the real question at hand.

I remember when I was in my late twenties and I had fallen deeply in love with a woman named Brenda. We had a very passionate one-year relationship. Brenda was sexy, smart, really funny, and when I was with her, my world was all smiles. After a year, Brenda had had enough of me, and the relationship came to a sudden end. I remember writing letters to her, imploring her to give us another chance. I sent flowers in an attempt to win her back. Finally, I had to realize that it was over. I was devastated. My dominant feeling was an intense fear of being alone and being profoundly sad. I was not hungry. I did not feel like working. Everything seemed dull and muted. My greatest fear at the time was realized. I was alone again.

I did something very wise back then. I did nothing. I did not run out to find another woman. I did not start drinking. I did not sit in front of the television. Instead, I took the advice of a wise old crone, and I took walks in nature. Whenever I got that sick to my stomach feeling, that overwhelming fear of being abandoned, I got up, and went to a park and walked. It was amazing how I could shift my feeling by joining in with nature. I did not feel alone amongst the oak trees. I did not feel alone watching the red tail hawks flying in the sky overhead. I did not feel alone when I smelled the sweetness of the rose bush or the jasmine.

The choice is to distract from the fear and avoid the situation, or feel the fear and move forward anyway. I have noticed over the years that those who try to avoid the fearful situation never do. That situation will continue to reappear until it is dealt with. You can run but you can't hide. And when that time comes, the time when I face the fear, feel the fear, and then take the appropriate action, I am free, even if only for that short amount of time. Each time I live with the fear and move forward, it gets easier, although I would say it never gets comfortable. This is the essential nature of the act of surrender. You have to give up. This is the beginning of learning to let it all go. This is the opening to the gates of heaven.

It is my experience that once the universe sees that you don't run and hide there will be rewards, and unexpected feelings and insights and gifts. Going back to my nature walks, I began to feel a strange oneness with everyone and everything. First I noticed a strong connection with the trees. It was as if I and the trees both acknowledged our antiquity, and the sharing of our mutual wisdom. My sensitivity to all elements of nature began to expand. I noticed the way the light shined through the canopy at noon. I noticed how the wind would blow the branches smooth one day, and then almost in circles another day. Other days, everything seemed so still, almost surreal. These are the types of gifts of which I speak. This was my first real demonstration of the phrase, "When the student is ready, the teacher will appear."

> *"I learned that courage was not the absence of fear, but the triumph over it. The brave man is not he who does not feel afraid, but he who conquers that fear."*

— Nelson Mandela

Unfortunately, many don't have these experiences. Rather than feel the fear, they run from it. They hide, acting as if the fear never existed. They drink. They medicate. They chase after sex. They eat and veg in front of the TV. The worst part of all of this is how it makes us feel. How do you feel when confronted with a fearful situation, and instead of taking a deep breath and moving forward, you run and hide? I feel like a coward. I feel like I ripped myself off. I feel a bit of self-loathing. I feel like I missed out on something. My aliveness takes a big hit. The magic dies.

Isn't it always fear that creates our feelings of separation? It is fear that creates you and me. If in the moment we are not feeling fear of anything, then we feel at one with everything and everyone. So simple. Yet all suffering is born out of a feeling of separation. If we are one with everything, we do not suffer.

I suggest doing something that goes against all I have been taught – Do nothing and feel the fear when it arises. Don't avoid fear and don't resist fear. Don't ignore the fear. Acknowledge it. Feel it. Own it. Let it burn you up. Think of fear as internal gasoline waiting to be lit to burn up more gunk. Or think of your fear as your greatest ally. Your fear is your greatest teacher. When fear appears, honor it. Know that the fear you feel is here only to teach you. Pretending it doesn't exist, pretending you don't feel it, pretending you don't have any fear, only makes it worse and increases your feelings of separation, which increases your suffering. To repeat something my Dad always said, "Honesty is the best policy." I AM AFRAID. You know when this is true. And when it is true for you, say it loud and strong, for that is the only way for a fully present human being to respond to fear.

The hardest part of the fear is to just let it be, acknowledge it and feel it. To acknowledge that we have fear makes us so human. We hate that, don't we? We'd rather be above it all, chosen ones, gifted leaders, unusually perceptive, and ever so special. Fear continues to point out our truth, which, I am sorry to say is that we aren't special. We are just like everyone else and we get afraid. We are all running scared. And, we all have the same choices. We can own up to the fear, and really feel it, or we can be phony and try to tell the world we aren't afraid and we don't have any fears. No one is going to believe this lie. It is your choice. Make it a wise one.

Feeling your fear will generate all the compassion you will ever need to be of service. And it will put you just at your edge, at your most awake, most creative, and most alive and present. By not resisting our fears, we feel them. And by feeling them, we transform while the fears gently begin to fade away. By feeling our fears, they burn through you and they burn away, sometimes slow and sometimes like a tinderbox aflame.

There is a universal wisdom, which honors honesty and courage. If you are honest with yourself, and courageous enough to feel deep into your fears, the universe seems to say "Well done." Out of the honesty and courage, your focus will begin to shift from your own personal fears and suffering, to a much larger perspective of fear and suffering. We begin to understand that the root of all fear begins with our fear of death. Once we realize we are infinite beings, and death is not an end, but rather a transformation, our relationship with fear takes on a whole new level of understanding. In learning to "know thyself" and get comfortably uncomfortable in our own skins, we are humbled and we become vulnerable. This is where true love lives. This is where the sacred is. This is the pathway to divine grace.

Assignment:

What are you afraid to do, but know that the doing of it will transform you? Do it. Do it now.

Step 26

Obstacles

"Our inward power, when it obeys nature, reacts to events by accommodating itself to what it faces - to what is possible. It needs no specific material. It pursues its own aims as circumstances allow; it turns obstacles into fuel.

The impediment to action advances action. What stands in the way becomes the way."

—Marcus Aurelius

Isn't it true that we feel the most alive, the most real, the most authentic, when we are going through the most challenging of times? Had a bout with cancer? Experienced the death of a loved one? Job loss? Relationship dissolution? Career change? Financial chaos? Stopping any form of intoxication (drinking, smoking, narcotics, gambling, debt, having sex etc.)? If you look at this honestly, the times of the greatest challenge, when life hardly seems worth living, when nothing else really matters, when depression may have set in, when staying in bed sounds as attractive as taking a walk along the beach, these are the times when you and I have been the closest to the true nature of our current incarnation. It is undeniable. Challenges wake us up.

There are a few major obstacles we must acknowledge on the path to radical freedom. The first obstacle is outside authority. We are raised with authority figures who get in our head and tell us what to do. The path of adult maturation demands that we think for ourselves. All authority must be assumed within. Outside authority must be systematically challenged, questioned and discarded. I must take full responsibility not only for my current life, but for my past life and the resulting behaviors and thought forms I have acquired. I bring this up because for most of us, we have been lied to from the day we were born. We have been told what to believe, how to live, what to pursue, and what will bring us happiness. How is that working for you? Do you enjoy being a cog in the wheel? Are you starting to ask questions, and are you beginning to figure things out on your own? In order to do that, one must assume full self-authority. At some point, giving over your authority to anyone else, or to any group, is anathema to your soul.

"Your time is limited, so don't waste it living someone else's life. Don't be trapped by dogma – which is living with the results of other people's thinking. Don't let the noise of others' opinions drown out your own inner voice. And most important, have the courage to follow your heart and intuition."

—Steve Jobs

So now as you read on, ponder on this. Is it not true for you that the times of greatest challenge, pain, and despondency were the most authentic experiences you have had? As I sit with the men in my groups, I can pretty quickly tell who is deep in a challenging life experience. He is not giddy with excitement about a new car. He is not talking about his latest sexual conquest. Nor is he ranting on about his woman and relationship. No, rather he is humbled. He is vulnerable. His heart is flayed wide open. He is authentic. He is seeing the world through new eyes. He is experiencing a death, and in that space, the seeds of a new existence are beginning to spring forth. He knows in that moment, that the car, the sex and the women, all that stuff, is fairly incidental to what really matters here and now. It is more the stuff of dreams. In fact, he is beginning to see that this life is a dream. He is experiencing the seeds of awakening. And for the first time, he may be actually living in the current moment, without regrets for the past and fears for the future.

The second obstacle that is planted firmly in our way is our reactions to our feelings. When we feel bad, it is common to want to change something so as to feel good again. We miss out on the gold nuggets. Why is it that when we feel lonely, despondent, depressed, humbled or vulnerable, we feel life to be the most real and authentic? Why is it that during these specific periods of time, we also feel that life is meaningless? This is very interesting. When we stop listening to the outside authorities telling us what is meaningful, and when we go through some of life's most challenging moments, we find life to be empty and meaningless. Let me restate that this is key. To be clear, during our most authentic moments, when we feel perfectly clear and present, life feels empty and meaningless. True? What do you think this means? This is a big question, the answer of which can have huge implications on your life. There is a huge freedom that comes from this seminal realization.

"The inner emptiness is the door to God."

—Osho

Now, whatever it means to you, this undeniable feeling that life is empty is something most of us do not like. It is scary. It gives one a feeling of being unhinged. It goes against most everything we have been taught. It is new and different, and most of us will do just about anything not to feel it. At first it feels wrong to be living a life that is empty and meaningless. As Morpheus showed Neo the stark sterile nature of the matrix, Neo uttered, "No, it can't be." Well, apparently it can be and it is. Adults face the music and walk through it. Children intoxicate and avoid. Adults experience the freedom of truth. Children prefer to live in lies.

The way most of us deal with these challenging feelings is to intoxicate ourselves. Think of all the ways we as humans intoxicate ourselves, all in an effort to banish the emptiness. The emptiness reminds us that death is coming. No matter how we live this life, no matter how well we love, no matter how much we give, nor how magnificently we live, we are going to exit this place. Death, there is no way around it. This truth lies at the core of every fear we have. That is what the little

165

bastard whispers in our ears. And so, to shut him up, we intoxicate on life. During most of my life I had been living in fear, obsessed with intoxicating and avoiding. I initially felt my little bastard when my first marriage was coming to an end. I felt miserable, depressed, suicidal, and trapped. Life did not feel worth living. What was the point? I had achieved those things on which I had set my sights. I had a good job, a wife, children, a house, all of the things I thought I had wanted. However, as I came to understand, there is an emptiness in acquisition. And so came the knock-knock on the door of my mind. The little bastard was ready to break the door down. I had to get out. I had to jump into the arms of another woman. I had to start smoking. I had to move. I had to get a new job. And with all those distractions, I was able to resume life in my own Technicolor dream for another 10 years. Funny how it all works…simple, yet very clever.

There is an emptiness in acquisition. After you have achieved something profound, or purchased a big ticket item, often the response to yourself is something like, "Is that all there is?" or, "Is that it?" or, "Hmmm?" There is an emptiness in acquisition. After fantastic sex and a mind-blowing orgasm, it does not take long for the little bastard to whisper in your ear, "That's it?" Notice how you feel after watching the Super Bowl. Right after the conclusion, there is an immediate let down. "Was that it?" There is a letdown after every intoxication because life does not match up to our illusory expectations. We strongly desire that life has some meaning, yet the truth of our feelings does not resonate commensurate with our desires.

Many men go fishing all of their lives without knowing that it is not fish they are after.

—Henry David Thoreau

A glorious and magnificent life is one that is lived in truth. The truth is that all these obstacles become a problem when we associate with our ego, and listen to the little bastard, take his advice, and react to discomfort. Most run from the truth, preferring to live in a sort of dream state rather than make the dedicated effort to understand this amazing life we are privileged to call home. As we embrace all of life, and not just the "good" stuff, have you noticed how life gets simpler? Fears abate. Synchronicity abounds. Mysteries unfurl. You begin to understand things from a much larger perspective. Everything starts to fit into a paradigm that makes sense of all situations. Unfortunately, you can't learn this stuff by reading about it. You must live it. You must learn to embrace all of it. You must walk through the obstacles and expose them for what they are. The payoff off is immediate and substantial. Your energy will rise. You will be humble. You will be vulnerable. You will be wildly attractive to both sexes. You will feel and recognize the interconnections of all beings. Life will become magical. And all of this is available, right now, just on the other side of this moment, by simply beginning to look at life honestly and on your own terms. It is your life. The invitation is to live it exceptionally.

Assignment:

Describe an obstacle in your life that seemed devastating, and explore how much you gained from the experience.

Step 27

Too Much Thinking

"Too much thinking can be a dangerous thing."

—Henri Cartier-Bresson

I think too much. At least, *I think* I think too much. In this regard, when I think of my childhood, I am saddened at the current state of my own internal affairs. I remember riding my bike, the wind blowing cool in my face, and pure adrenaline excitement pumping through my veins. I didn't stress over the height of the curb. I didn't give a thought to my physical condition and how I would make it all the way to the grocery store and back. I never considered the possibility of a car wiping me out. Truly, as I look back, given all the amazing and often life threatening experiences I had, I must have been doubly blessed by angels. Where did the angels go? Where did those experiences go? Where did I go?

It truly is an accomplishment, and even more so for men, to retain our childlike qualities. Wonderful timeless qualities such as curiosity, wonder, innocence, and passion in the moment come to mind. I recently saw an interview of the French photographer, Henri Cartier-Bresson, who is considered the greatest photographer of the twentieth century. What a life he led. He spoke about his experiences traveling the world, engaging in conversations with Henri Matisse and Picasso. I particularly noticed one statement he made. Twice, during the interview, he said, "Thinking can be a dangerous thing." Not once, but twice! This concept was something he had obviously come to grips with early on in his life. He kept talking about the subtle textures of the life experience, and how his job as a photographer was to feel when the moment was right to click his camera. He repeatedly said it was all about feel as he gently rubbed his fingers together.

It is important here to make a fine distinction. The statement, "Thinking can be a dangerous thing," is not an absolute. It is conditional. Certainly, no one is implying we should all stop thinking. That is absurd. Thinking also allows us to achieve many valuable experiences in life. For most of us, we think all the time. At work, we think. At home, we think. When there is a problem to be worked out, we think. Our left-brains are fully engaged most of the time. We use our thinking to survive and ensure the survival and abundance of our partners and children. So what is so dangerous about it?

Let's qualify this statement as follows: When it comes to matters of the heart, thinking can be a very dangerous thing. When we think, we often disconnect from our hearts, and that can be dangerous. It's not the life and death kind of dangerous. It's the kind of dangerous that can have you marry one man out of security, rather than marrying a man who inspires you, challenges you, and perhaps can scare you. Your mind will tell you to take the secure route. Not much passion, but very secure. Your heart tells you to go for it, create a life of daily intercourse and depth. Take a risk and live a little. Here, thinking can be a very dangerous thing.

For Henri Cartier-Bresson, his work as a photographer was a matter of the heart. All his senses were extremely fine-tuned. He felt his photographs in the air. He saw with his eyes, but his magic was his intuition and his feeling. He could feel in his body when the right time was approaching. He said, "I don't take photographs, the photographs take me." With this approach, no thinking is necessary. Just feel, hold on and let the experience take you wherever it will. I am sure this is true for all great artists. They aren't creating anything. Something much bigger is being created through them. The great artists become the catalyst for the creations to occur. Clearly, thinking has no place in this magical process. Does thinking have much of a place in the magical process of your life?

Is your life a magical process? Or is it a calculated, measured approach to achieve maximum benefit? I know this is true for me. I am frustrated by the amount of thinking I do. I feel at times like my brain is going to melt down. I now see my children and marvel at how natural and spontaneous they are. Or, when I am with a woman, and I feel my heart open, my mind immediately wants to weigh in on the situation, and stop the natural flow of my self-expression. My mind creates fear. My mind reminds me of past hurts. "You don't want to go there again!" I am thinking once again. The moment of fiery passion has been doused with cold water. White smoke billows out of my being.

Yes, thinking can be a dangerous thing. Thinking can kill your spirit at each turn along the way. You may live a successful life. You may have lived a secure life. You may have a nice house, nice car, and nice family. But did you really live? Did thinking hold you back from the real magic? Did your passions express themselves? Did you survive without really living? These types of questions scare me to my core. I don't know about you, but I don't want to look back with regrets. I refuse to let fear stop me from really living. I refuse to be the logical and linear thinking being that my society seems so intent on producing.

There are no straight lines in nature. It is all curves, waves, flow, back and forth, in and out. As a boy, I was taught to set my sights on a goal, and then march straight forward to achieve that goal. Then I was to set another goal. I suppose this was to go on till the end of my days. As a fifty something man, my experience doesn't correspond with this model. My most wonderful and memorable moments have occurred when I veered off the path. In the ditches and the side roads, that is where the juice has been. When I did veer off the path, I wasn't thinking too much. My guts, my instincts led me on a different path. It was pure experience. "Off Roading" can be a blast!

Living with intuition as my guide requires a surrender. I know people who have surrendered and they are alive. And I know even more people who are the walking dead. Yes, blood is pumping through their heart, but there isn't anything else pumping through. Walk along a busy city street and you will see the walking dead in droves. Little eye contact and even less life force. I feel this is the effect of too much thinking. Too much thinking seems to numb us out. It is like we forget what it is like to feel. And since these moments of feeling are so distant and unknown, we get scared of them and do everything we can to ignore them. It is no surprise that in our culture, alcohol, cigarettes and drug abuse continue to run rampant. Numb the feelings, numb the pain, and numb the ecstasy. And still, the trees try to speak with us. Why isn't anyone listening?

So what do you do with an overactive thinking mechanism? It would seem that recognizing the situation and committing to a life of more feeling is the first step. I find myself increasingly drawn to situations I can't figure out. I am drawn to matters of the spirit and the lives of mystics. I participate in group events that produce a tangible energy I can feel. Then I remember, bit by bit, what I am here to do. I keep jumping back into the fire, to feel the fire, and keep some of the fire in my heart. If only we can stop thinking about how to get more than we give. If only everyone realized the more they give, the more they have.

Life is a creation. Creation can't be planned. When I sit down to start writing, I have very little idea of what will come out of my fingers. I sit down with my MacBook Pro on my lap. I pick some music, plug in my ear buds, and see where it takes me. It's not neat. It's not predictable. If I am going to do my best work, it is going to come from a place beyond thought and reason and predictability. It is going to arise out of nowhere, and my job is to be the clearing for it all to show up, capture it, mold it a bit, and then present it for consumption. It works best when I do very little thinking.

Assignment:

I wish I could tell you to stop thinking for an hour. It doesn't work that way. All we can do is become more cognizant of the phenomenon. So think all you like. Work to notice when you let the thinking make decisions for you rather than listening to your inner voice.

Step 28

Opening My Eyes

"Like a sculptor, if necessary,
carve a friend out of stone.
Realize that your inner sight is blind
and try to see a treasure in everyone."

— Rumi

I was twenty-two when I began working at Leo Burnett, a prestigious advertising agency located in Chicago, Illinois. It was my first corporate job, a prize I had earned as a college graduate. I still remember getting dressed each day, proudly tying my power tie, and then catching the green and white bus that motored past Lake Superior and down Michigan Avenue. Being a native Californian, it was quite a shift in my life: new job, new city, and new friends. Life was vibrant and rich.

I was in the account executive training program with fifty or so other new college graduates from around the country. We worked ourselves to the bone in either the media or research department before getting promoted to the job of assistant account executive. It was a competitive environment, as you can imagine, with all of us doing our best to deliver on the bold promises we made during our job interviews. It was during one of many meetings we attended that I heard a senior executive make a statement I have never forgotten.

As aspiring executive wannabes, we were trying to create a dynamic new media campaign for one of our clients. We had changed one core component that had delivered very well for the past 5 years. We were asked about this change to the plan and didn't have much of an answer, other than to say we wanted to try something different. The senior executive then stated what now seems like a fairly obvious truth: "If it ain't broke, don't fix it." I now look back on that statement as a profound truth because there is something inside us that wants to fix things, even when they are not broken. Let's call that certain something that lives inside of me, The Fixer, a unique aspect of ourselves that we can use to our benefit or detriment.

Let me tell you about The Fixer. First of all, he is a determined fellow. No matter what, he wants to fix. The Fixer loves a good problem. The harder the problem, the happier The Fixer! Without a problem, The Fixer tends to fade into the background. However, make no mistake; The Fixer is not going to give up. If there is no problem, The Fixer will more often than not create a problem just to keep himself occupied. One target that The Fixer places a big bull's-eye is on a woman. Many men have a strong desire to fix their woman in a misguided attempt to make their own lives better. I hear it all the time: "She is too emotional." "She is not passionate enough." "She is too independent." "I wish she would have more of a life outside of our relationship." The blame game is alive and well.

The pertinent question here is – Why does she have to be anything different than she is? She is not broken, so why do you want to fix her? I suggest that if you are trying to fix your woman, you have not fully settled into your masculine core. Whatever dissatisfaction you are feeling about your woman is your dissatisfaction. Rather than trying to fix something that is already complete and whole, begin to work on that part of you that doesn't feel complete and whole, with or without a woman.

A man who is fully settled into his masculine essence realizes that his woman, among many things, is in part a brilliant reflection of himself. She is your mirror. And if you don't like the image you are getting back, the answer does not lie in breaking the mirror and then trying to glue all the pieces back together. Instead, going deep within yourself is the place to put your focus. Anytime we look to external sources for our gratification, we are in trouble. We can't change or fix most external forces. For the most part, life is loose and out of control. When it is time for your transmission to break, it will break. Time for the flu, so be it. Life throws us all kinds of curve balls. As men, we have a choice to observe and respond to what is happening all around us and marvel at the mysterious and magical nature of it all, or we can get frustrated and angry and place blame. Are you a man or a child?

At this point, some men may be screaming at me, "She really is a nasty person and I can't stand her!" OK, OK, I do understand that not all matches are made in heaven. But if that is the case and she really is horrid, why are you with a woman who brings out such virulent feelings? Fish or cut bait. There is no point in straddling the fence. You have a choice. Choose her as your woman, exactly as she is, or leave her and wish her well. If you are in that place of evaluating your options, and there doesn't seem to be a clear answer, you are probably with the right woman for you for now. She is challenging you, reflecting your deepest truths and wounds, and whether you realize it or not, you honor the internal growth she fosters in you. Painful? Sure. You get angry? Of course. But ultimately, you chose each other for just that reason. The relationship serves you both by exposing those dark issues of yourselves you probably would not have seen without sharing a life together. Out of the darkness comes those crystalline moments of clarity and bliss and transformation.

I know men that have been with the same woman for ten to fifteen years, pecking at their own chests, suffering while waiting for their women to change. At some point, the suffering becomes so great that a stark realization takes hold. "Why am I doing this to myself?" "She isn't going to change." And in that moment of realization, you may choose her exactly as she is. This was my experience. It was like a breath of fresh air. Once I made the choice to accept a woman as is, she transformed as if by miracle. But in "reality" she didn't change. I changed. And in that moment, the whole world changed as well.

Don't expect your woman to change. She won't. It is a sure formula for thwarted feelings and frustration. She isn't broken. And she doesn't deserve your judgment or condemnation. She certainly does not deserve the self-righteous feeling coming from you that she isn't good enough as she is. You would have to be as thick as a plank not to see how this is your story and not her story. It is time to be responsible for your own feelings of self-worth, and stop projecting them upon the world and specifically upon your intimate partner.

It is a challenge to find a man who truly respects the wisdom of women. Most men, mired in the pathology of patriarchy, can't see clearly through the darkened lens. Until a man surrenders to the power/divine connection/creative force of a woman (any woman, not necessarily his partner) and is humbled by the living goddess within the feminine form, he will hold women as a second-class citizen. Social conditioning makes it so.

Women, on the other hand, in order to warrant said respect, must do the heavy lifting to find and nurture the goddess within. European women do this better than our American sisters. Sadly, many women simply do not know of the power they wield. Therefore they invite the patriarchal dismissal, unaware that a man in their life is a choice and not a result of need.

Women living fully within their power are the most beautiful beings in creation. Only a humble man will ever experience the joy of co-creating with the feminine in a true organic partnership. How can we expect women to blossom into their full radiance when they are being told, directly and indirectly, they aren't good enough? Constant pressuring to become a new and improved version of themselves only leads to resistance and despondency and retraction. Don't look out. Look within. And after many sessions of deep introspection, you may realize that The Fixer is just The Trickster in disguise. The truth is, you don't need to be fixed either. It is all just a ruse to challenge you and keep you distracted and off purpose. The Fixer is just one of many personas of the ego. When you realize he doesn't need to exist, you pass. When you take responsibility for your own experience, life begins to show up as a synchronistic symphony of glorious moments. You will wonder where you have been hiding all this time. And the woman who has patiently been waiting for you to appear will show up again as the goddess she has always been.

Assignment:

Select someone in your life, be it man or woman, and ask for permission to share just how much you value them in your life. If you feel comfortable, and they feel comfortable, tell them all the qualities you appreciate (and would never try to change). Make someone's day, and make your own at the same time. Be generous.

Step 29

Synchronicity

"According to Vedanta, there are only two symptoms of enlightenment, just two indications that a transformation is taking place within you toward a higher consciousness. The first symptom is that you stop worrying. Things don't bother you anymore. You become light-hearted and full of joy. The second symptom is that you encounter more and more meaningful coincidences in your life, more and more synchronicities. And this accelerates to the point where you actually experience the miraculous."

— Deepak Chopra

Swiss psychologist Carl Jung first began using the word synchronicity in the 1920s to describe the experience of two seemingly unrelated events happening in a manner that is meaningful. The disparate events, when combined in time and space, create a sort of "Aha moment." The relationship of meaning is sufficient in and of itself to constitute synchronicity, and it is not necessary to find some causal relationship between the events.

It is a phenomenon in which separate events are seen as related, or connected, although there is no cause and effect in the normal meaning of the phrase. As one begins to expand his or her consciousness, it become self-evident that people and things are much more interconnected than we might normally observe. Some take that one step further and feel everything is composed of just one element, energy, and as a result, everything is connected to everything else. This type of perception leads to an ever-growing awareness of synchronicity.

Synchronicity is a sign that you are on a true life path. When things start to merge and connect, and you begin to see the underlying relationship of people and events, this is a good sign you are breaking through old concepts of reality, and are starting to see the world as it truly is.

In 2005, I had an experience that could only be described in terms of synchronicity. I had read a book called *Of Water and the Spirit* by Malidoma Some. In that book, Some introduced me to a few of the initiation rituals of the Dagara tribe in Africa. I became particularly interested in the burial ritual. In this ritual, the young boys who were to be initiated into manhood dug a hole in the ground. The hole could either be horizontal, like a traditional burial site, or vertical, so the boy could stand in the hole, allowing dirt to be added up to his neck. In either case, the boy was stuck in the ground up to his neck, unable to free himself of his own accord. This ritual became a key component of the men's weekends I have been conducting for the past 10 years.

About this same time, I discovered a book called *The Shamanic Way of the Bee*. This book chronicles the relationship between an initiate and an apprentice. The mentor and those of his tribe have studied and revere the honeybee. The book is a discourse on the value of living one's life in accordance with the ways of the honeybee. It is a fascinating book, and I recall be fully engaged through and through. Unbelievably, at the end of the book, the initiate leads the apprentice through yet another burial ritual (you wouldn't think there were that many burial rituals!). This ritual is a bit more intense than the Dagara ritual. In the Shamanic Way of the Bee ritual, the participant is laid flat in a horizontal hole in the ground, and then set up with a tub with which to breathe, and some beeswax to cover this ear, eyes, and nose. Then the dirt is placed on top until covered completely. The participant is to lie there over night, unable to move or free himself until dug up the following morning. Just the thought of this ritual sends shivers up my spine.

This is an example of synchronicity. I became interested in burial rituals. I searched out one book. And then, out of nowhere, I found myself reading another book that also spoke in detail about a burial ritual. There are not too many books on the topic. Yet they both found their way to me. While this is a fine example of synchronicity, it is the not the most profound example. What happened next is even more unusual. Even as I recall the incident, I can't begin to fathom how it happened.

I was driving into Santa Rosa, CA to have a guy look at my windshield. It had been cracked, and I was getting an estimate for a replacement. Now as I said, I was reading about the honeybee in the book *The Shamanic Way of the Bee*. I arrived at my destination, parked in the shade, and got out of my car. It was a hot day, so I made sure all the windows were closed. I had run the air conditioning, and wanted to keep all the cold air inside the car. I was in meeting with the windshield guy, getting the quote, going over the logistics, etc., and returned to my car some 15 minutes later. I got in my car, started it up, and began to drive home. About half way home I felt a sharp pain in the center of my upper back. I lessened the pressure of my body on the seat, and continued to drive. The pain did not go away, so I pulled over to see if I could figure out what was going on back there, and remedy the situation.

Now this is synchronicity. As I got out of the car, there on the driver's seat was a dead honeybee. I had been stung by a honeybee, in my car, while I was driving home. I was dumbfounded. There was no way a bee could have gotten in my car, let alone end up at the midpoint of my back, and then sting me. But it did. Clearly, something much bigger was at play with me as the recipient of this unique confluence of events. I read one book, which then led me to another book. The second book is all about honeybees. And then, for the first time in my life, a bee stung me in my car, on a day in which I had my windows shut.

Synchronicities can be fascinating. They can even seem miraculous. It is easy to get distracted by the apparent mystical nature of intertwined events. However, synchronicities are simply a sign, or a threshold, which one experiences to provide further verification that things are not always as they seem. As you begin to broaden your perception, and release the tiller of control over your life, you will find that synchronicities abound. Everything truly is connected.

How many times have you thought about a particular friend, and then that friend calls you on the telephone? How many times have you been thinking about a scene from a movie, and then you find that movie playing on the television? Noticing and creating minor synchronicities such as this is one way the universe is telling you you're progressing nicely down a path toward greater awareness and consciousness.

Assignment:

Recall a special or unique moment in your life. Recall many if you have more than one. Allow yourself to be amazed at the magic that is everywhere.

Step 30

Pleasure

"I don't know why we are here, but I'm pretty sure that it is not in order to enjoy ourselves."

—Ludwig Wittgenstein

While this quote may be true in the grand scheme of things, and there are certainly many painful roads to traverse on our way to any real awakening, experiencing pleasure is certainly a fundamental component of any fully integrated human being. Many of our earliest memories are of experiences that provided us with pleasure, but when discovered or observed by others, we were admonished, scolded, punished or even physically threatened or harmed. It is the nature of someone who is not experiencing pleasure, to react strongly and negatively to someone who is experiencing pleasure. We all have our wounds.

Sexual pleasure has been an impactful issue in my life. And by sex, I am not only referring the sex act, but also physical intimacy, touch, relating to the opposite sex, and my potency as a man. I was raised with clear instructions that sex before marriage is a sin, masturbation is a sin, and doing either would no doubt send me straight to hell. That type of religious programming can really do a number on a young boy, and it certainly did a douzy on me.

I have been quite an expert on how to live a life with little pleasure, or more accurately stated, pleasure followed by feelings of guilt and shame. Even when I had moments of joy and pleasure, very quickly, thoughts of shame and guilt would flood my being. Even with all the personal development work I had done on myself, this issue of allowing myself pleasure, of allowing myself to receive, of allowing someone else to give to me, was one of the final hurdles I needed to jump if I was ever going to be truly free.

This inability to freely enjoy pleasure showed up in my life as a sexual dysfunction, primarily premature ejaculation. To be in a man's body, and not have control of his ejaculation, this is a tough road to walk. When a man knows he cannot truly pleasure a woman with his penis, he walks the Earth somewhat limp, weak and not fully integrated. Premature ejaculation is a rampant dysfunction, as most any woman will tell you. Depending on the medical source, the average length of intercourse is in the 5-minute range. However the ideal length of time is from 7 to 12 minutes for mutual pleasure. There is quite a bit of lousy, unfulfilling sex occurring worldwide.

It wasn't until I realized how much this issue was impacting how I was feeling about myself and how I was experiencing my life that I got to the heart of the matter lickety-split. I knew I would need the assistance of an experienced female guide, and I am grateful I was able to find a woman with the title of Dakini. Dakini means "sky dancer" in Tibetan and is described as a dazzling enchantress who soars through clouds, reveling in utmost freedom. The dakini I engaged was a woman who was willing to work with a client to explore the world of physical pleasure, and help to unblock those kinks that prevent or inhibit pleasure. During the course of several sessions, I came right up against my shame and guilt around sexual activity. As with any issue, I had to feel the pain, and experience the fear of falling short with women (aka performance anxiety), and push through it rather than avoid it. I had to understand how my sexual dysfunction served me in the past, but now was no longer necessary. I am pleased to report the patient was cured.

I am very grateful for any women who undertake the role of sex worker or sex therapist, for I know first hand of the great masculine pain that is present in the sexual arena. You don't have to look very far to see that we are a world that is made crazy around sex. Rapes, domestic violence, unsatisfying sex, divorce, all point to a world that seems incapable of freely enjoying pleasure and taking responsibility for our sexuality.

Having thoroughly dealt with my own dysfunction, and now able to enjoy and revel in my sexual experiences, I can say the journey through the pain was well worth the effort. To see love making as a dance, rather than a performance, is transformational. To feel control of my body, and to know I can surrender to sensual experiences, and truly let go to give and receive pleasure, has changed everything for me. I walk with a confidence I never had, and see the world as one big ongoing opportunity to play and engage. I also smile quite a bit more now!

What it came down to was this question: "Do I deserve it?" Do I deserve to live a fully experienced life, one with not a single false belief, one with not a single filter, and one with not a single experience shrouded by my past? Do I deserve to live in the present moment, alive, open, and raw? For most of my life, the answer was a tacit no. Now it is a big yes. I do deserve it all, and why not! How about you?

For many, this entire conversation may make you uncomfortable, and I suggest that is something to look at. We can't even talk about sex in most circumstances without thinking it is inappropriate. If we can't even talk about it, how are we supposed to explore it, heal from it and enjoy it? The bottom line is there is a sensual nature to our human condition. We have a minimum of five senses, all of which are capable of profound joy and pleasure. The invitation is to break through any blockages keeping you from requesting that for which your heart yearns. And once you have it, the invitation is to enjoy it free of shame and guilt. Party on, Garth!

187

Assignment:

Go and feel pleasure. Maybe start simply by getting a massage. Or go and enjoy one of Baskin Robbins' 31 flavors. Can you relax and fully enjoy it? That is the invitation of this step.

Step 31

Shame

"Suffering has been stronger than all other teaching, and has taught me to understand what your heart used to be. I have been bent and broken, but - I hope - into a better shape."

— Charles Dickens

So now we are really getting to the real stuff, the nitty gritty. Let go to where most all of us began: childhood. I was raised a Catholic. Seems Catholics are famous for, among other things, guilt. Catholics are good about feeling guilty. As I look back, I realized I was told about a whole bunch of rules. There were so many rules, there was no way I could live and not break quite a few of them. I guess the idea is then I would feel guilty for not following all the rules. Then I would have to go to church to pray for forgiveness and attend confession and take communion to be purified and ready for a new week. That didn't work for me, so I just stopped being a Catholic at the age of 30. It still seems like a rigged system.

Guilt appears to result from something we have done which we judge as "bad." I put bad in quotation marks because calling something "bad" is a judgment, and not a statement of fact. This is an important point. The same applies to a judgment we call "good." It is not a statement of fact, but rather a self-imposed judgment, or a label we apply, to an event, a thing, a feeling, an emotion, or a person.

"The location of the dividing line between the concepts of shame, guilt, and embarrassment is not fully standardized. Psychoanalyst Helen B. Lewis

argued that, 'The experience of shame is directly about the self, which is the focus of evaluation. In guilt, the self is not the central object of negative evaluation, but rather the thing done is the focus.' Similarly, Fossum and Mason say in their book Facing Shame that, 'While guilt is a painful feeling of regret and responsibility for one's actions, shame is a painful feeling about oneself as a person.'"

—Wikipedia

Guilt is a judgment about actions we have or haven't taken, and shame is a judgment about you and me as people. Either way, the point I want to make is that both are self-imposed judgments that cause us sadness and misery, and zaps us of our life force. These judgments then impact how we live our life, and create a filter through which we see and experience who we are and how we respond to everyday opportunities.

I know people, lots of people, who have shared in circles in which I was a participant. These are beautiful people, people who would not harm anyone or anything, people who truly care about other people. Still, something happened, something bad, something unforeseen, something they carry around like a battle scar, something that shadows how they live. No intentional damage. Not anything like, "I set out to do harm." No, just something happened, and from that point on, these beautiful people feel guilty.

"What is seen as right and normal by society is seen as immature distortion by a free mind."

—Vernon Howard

All this guilt seems to be a result of early conditioning, whether it is from religion, or some other source, which creates these ridiculously high expectations of how perfect we should all be able to live our lives. What I want to say is, "Lighten up! You are doing the best you can. Enjoy it all!" I realize my words are like farts in the wind. An adult who has been told how to live his life, and which rules to follow since birth, isn't going to change with a simple suggestion. These ideas are too deeply ingrained. It is all too orchestrated. The tribe is in agreement. That is the way it is going to be. But just maybe a few people might be moved to be a bit less tough on themselves, and realize you aren't a bad person, you are doing the best you can, and life really is about being free, and uncontrolled. Why aren't we able to evaluate our actions without anyone else's guidance? Perhaps just one person may reclaim their authority, and not give it away. Just maybe it's you.

Self-sabotage is what happens when we feel guilt and shame. Since we feel guilty, we convince ourselves we don't deserve the amazing life that has been offered to us. Instead, we find ways to accept less, go for less, and come up with all sorts of reasons why we don't have an amazing life, amazing love, amazing people, and amazing experiences. Instead, we see ourselves as bad people, or irresponsible people, or somehow undeserving people, and we screw it up for ourselves. Usually, it is my observation that most don't even see themselves doing it. Instead, it is just the way it is. We learn to settle for less, and accept that this is our lot in life. How do we free ourselves up from ourselves, from these self-imposed prisons and stop self-sabotaging?

What we must do is take out the garbage. Guilt and shame are bad habits. I suggest we can change our way of being. Burn your guilt. See what happens. In the end, it is all smoke anyway.

Assignment

Here is a great process or exercise that I will share with you. Write down all the things you feel guilty about. Take your time, and write down everything. Close your eyes for 15 minutes and see what comes up. Write it all down on a piece of paper. Then one night, when you feel ready to let it all go, just as the sun goes down, put the paper in a bowl and light it on fire. The next step is very important. Sit there and watch the paper burn. As you are watching it, feel the guilt lifting from your body. Imagine these clouds of guilt, in the form of smoke, lifting up to the sky. Just let them go. Feel whatever emotions you feel.

Many people feel sadness during this process, for they have grown comfortable with their guilt. Think about it. Without the excuse of guilt, what kind of a life are you going to build for yourself? This can be kind of scary. Has the guilt impacted your decisions about the work you do, the relationships you are in, and the activities you participate in daily? If you didn't feel guilty, would you treat your body better, and eat healthier food? Would you maybe stop smoking, and start exercising? It is a powerful experience to realize all the pernicious ways guilt thwarts us in life.

Step 32

What's Your Game?

"Each man had only one genuine vocation - to find the way to himself....His task was to discover his own destiny - not an arbitrary one - and to live it out wholly and resolutely within himself. Everything else was only a would-be existence, an attempt at evasion, a flight back to the ideals of the masses, conformity and fear of one's own inwardness."

— Hermann Hesse

My life has been lived with one predominant question in mind: "What's going on here?" I see the world and wonder if we are all crazy, following rules that were set up by someone else. It seems that very few stop the insanity and ask the question, "Hey, what the hell am I doing here on Earth?" It looks from my perspective as if we are a race of sheep, one following the other, with no real direction, simply moving forward, step by agonizing step, toward an uncertain destination. Ultimately, we are all marching toward our death. But in between birth and death, what are you up to? I ask myself, is there anything truly worth working toward besides security, power, children, fame, glory, stability, or life everlasting in heaven?

Isn't this type of questioning the most logical step in our development? We find ourselves in these human bodies, yet it seems clear we have a spirit, or a soul, or an energy that inhabits our bodies. We live in an objective reality that gives the appearance of a *you* and a *them*. This state has been referred to as duality. There is me and I am separate from you. Yet many of us have had the experience of feeling a oneness with everything, be it a religious experience, a connection with another human being, or a special walk along the beach. All of this raises the question, "What's going on here?" I have seen many people experience a glimpse of this oneness, but it doesn't last long because the idea of oneness is so foreign, and is not shared by others. It takes an incredible strength to hold on to the idea of oneness, or non-duality, and continue to investigate the truth of our existence regardless of commonly held beliefs. It is easier to be a sheep. Sad to say, most go the easy route. I have feared the unknown, and it will stop you in your tracks unless you have a clear picture of where you are going.

What's your game? Before looking at the most common games, or paths we all choose to live, it is important to note that underlying most games is fear. If your greatest fear is being broke and homeless, then your game will be all about security. If your greatest fear is going to hell, then your game will be about living a good life, abiding by the Ten Commandments, proselytizing, and giving to charity, all in an effort to avoid hell. What I have discovered is that all fear lives in a life unexamined. However, most never take the time to examine their lives. As you are reading this book, you are taking some time to examine your life, and for that I applaud you. Still, 99.99% don't. Rather than look at the source of the fear, it appears easier to change the outside circumstances of our lives, and thereby put the fear off to the side. The fear still lives strong, and to me, this seems a silly waste of a life.

Security. This seems to be the game most are playing. Our entire social structure is built upon achieving financial security. When I am with "normal" people at a gathering, say for example, a Fourth of July barbeque, the talk centers around the economy, vacillating real estate values, the unemployment rate, and jobs. The first question one man often asks another is, "So, Jay, what do you do for a living?" This is often followed by questions like, "Where do you live? Do you rent or own? How is your 401K doing?" Then the conversation tends to move to sports, and how the 49ers or the Giants are doing this year.

I know these conversations run rampant across this country. Think back on your last conversations in a social setting, and I am sure you will see the pattern. Now when your game is about discovering the truth, all of this financial talk seems a massive waste of time. Changing your game will change your perception of the world around you. I used to lead a men's group. We would get together every week on Tuesday evening for 3 hours. We'd talk about these deeper questions, and how they related to our relationships to work, women, and our families. One week, the men were given an assignment to engage another human being and change the course of the conversation to something less superficial, and with greater depth. This was a tough assignment. It takes courage to express anything of a vulnerable nature. For not only are you exposing yourself, but you run the risk of being rejected.

Not surprisingly, most men reported that once they opened the door to a topic of conversation more significant than the real estate market, the other man was often yearning to share and open himself up as well. The question of "What's going on?" lives within us all. It is a burning question that for most is never brought to the surface. But it is undeniably there, in existence, waiting to be explored, if only another will courageously breach the subject.

Power. This is another game played across the world. For many, security is not enough. We strive for the power to control others, be it as a high paid executive, CEO, or politician. I believe we have all seen, in the recent near collapse of our financial system, the role greed plays in this game. Again, remember that it is deep seated fear that drives the game. If you fear loss, then your game will be all about protecting yourself from the feeling of loss. Achieving great power and control will alleviate the feeling of the fear of loss. But make no mistake; the fear is still there, getting stronger each day. Playing the power game does not alleviate the fear, it only covers it up.

When I operate from a place of fear, I suffer. In many ways, the search for truth is a search for an end to suffering. The search for truth is a search for understanding. It is a search for an understanding of the mechanism that creates the fear. Rather than spending my life trying to cover up the fear, I have chosen to spend my life looking deep within myself (or within my self) to find some answers about why I and we are all so fearful. What is at the root of all this fear?

Another game commonly played across the world is the game I call Living a Good Life. As a child, I learned about God, the ten commandments, heaven and hell. I learned all the rules about attending church once a week, abstaining from premarital sex, and not eating meat on Fridays. At one point in my early years, I even considered becoming a priest. Many children are raised this way, told as fact, how the world works. As children, we still haven't learned the art of analysis and questioning. We have not reached the age of discrimination. And so, most take these beliefs and carry them throughout a lifetime. America is a Christian nation. In God we trust, and all that. It is very comfortable to be a part of the Christian tribe.

The fear of those who play the game of living a good life is hell: hell on Earth, and hell in the afterlife. There is a belief amongst Christians that if they live a good life, God, like an all-powerful parent, will grace them with security and abundance. Have you noticed how many people thank God upon winning a sports competition or winning an award? That acknowledgment of God is just another way to deflect the fear of loss. If I thank God first, then I will keep on winning. God is used like a lucky rabbit's foot. It is a clear manipulation. And if there is a God, I wonder how God feels about all this? He seems to be responsible for a bunch of people winning awards. Do you think God has a trophy case in heaven? If he does, it must be really big.

This step invites you to learn more about yourself. What is your game? This is a powerful question. The answer can show you how and why your life looks like it does. The question leads to clarity about what drives you and what you value most in your life. It can also point to fears and insecurities that underlie your actions. If you don't like your answer, you can always change your game.

Assignment:

What drives you? What is it that is your main driving force?
Acknowledge it regardless of what it is. What is your game? Ask
yourself if this the best game for you to be playing in order to live the
life you want to live.

Step 33

Ritual – Create a System

"The first draft of anything is shit."

—Ernest Hemingway

It is in the doing of something over and over again that we begin to achieve mastery. Malcolm Gladwell is famous for saying that it takes 10,000 of "deliberate practice" to become a master at anything. While practice may not make perfect, it certainly give us the opportunity to become better at what we are doing. Therefore, ritual is of vital importance on this journey to radical freedom. By ritual, I mean doing certain things on a regular, recurring basis. I could have named this section "Scheduling," but that eliminates the sacred nature of many tasks. Living with ritual in your life will help you to achieve several goals. First, it will allow you to be far more efficient with your time. Second, ritual will free up energy, as you will not have to debate day in and day out what you plan to do for the day. Third and most important, ritual slowly trains your ego to respect your true self. When your ego understand that your schedule is the law, the chattering will stop, and you will more easily connect with your inner voice, your inner wisdom and your intuition. And finally, ritual allows for mastery of your chosen pursuits.

There are certain things I must do each day. When I say must, I base that on the observation that when I don't do those things, my day does not show up the same. There is a way I like my day to show up, and there are very specific levers I know to pull to get the results. Here is my short list. These are the must-do items. I must work on my Internet marketing business. I must write. I must exercise. I must meditate. I must eat well, which for me is a high protein, low carb diet. I must have one good personal conversation with a close friend or family member. I must have some time allocated to doing nothing. Now that I have my list, I do not need to debate each day about what I plan to do. It's already figured out. All I have to concern myself with is doing what is on my agenda. Since these items all serve to empower me, and brighten my day, and raise my energy, and challenge me, every day is a day for joy.

"To enjoy life, you don't need fancy nonsense, but you do need to control your time and realize that most things just aren't as serious as you make them out to be."

—Timothy Ferriss

There was a moment when something just clicked for me. I remember setting up my daily schedule, looking at it, and saying to myself, "all I need to do is do these things." It really is that simple. Prioritize what you should be doing to achieve your most important goals, create a system to manage your time, and then consistently take action. It is not glamorous. It is not fancy nonsense. It is applying disciplined action to create an amazing life.

While achieving a state of radical freedom is wonderful, and freeing our minds from the false beliefs we have been carrying around is enlightening, I also feel the need to provide a very practical application. Chop Wood and Carry Water! If we are going to get anything done, and move toward our goals, we need a systemized and measureable approach. Let's get about the task of controlling what many consider our most valuable asset, time. It is time to create a simple life management system.

This is my system. I use 2 tools to manage my time. First I use a Google calendar to manage my time blocks. Those time blocks consist of 7 elements:

F – Free Time. This is time with absolutely no agenda. Let your mind run wild. All thoughts are welcome here. There is nothing to do. There is no place to be. You and your time are free.

R – Results Time. This is your work time. This is when you produce results.

E – Exercise Time. This is focused time for your body.

E – Edge Time. This is an activity that puts you at your edge. It is an activity that makes you uncomfortable. But you do it because it pushes you, and it creates aliveness in your energy body.

D – Divulge Time. This is time in which I am allowing myself to be vulnerable and share feelings and emotions. This could be in a conversation, or more often for me, it is expressed in my words and videos.

O – Outdoors Time. Go outside and experience nature. Rain or shine. Feel the outdoors. It is marvelous for your spirit, and you will be surprised how many great ideas are birthed out of a walk in nature.

M – Meditation Time – If you don't meditate, I recommend giving it a try. If you have meditated, I recommend adding it as a key component of your daily schedule. Some people start their day with it. I find meditation serves me best mid day, much like a rejuvenation period at the half time of my day.

Now you don't have to utilize all of the same elements that I do. If you do, you will notice these elements spell out Freedom, which is easy to remember. I recommend you try it out for a coupe of weeks and see how it goes. Regardless of the elements, the important thing is to create the system, and then surrender to it. You can take your elements and schedule them in a manner that works for you. For example, my early morning time is the best time for me to dive into my results time or work time. I knock out 4 hours before 8AM. Once you can surrender to the schedule, then you are free to perform at maximum capacity within the system. You will marvel at what you can get accomplished.

3:30 AM – Up. Shower. Coffee. Protein Shake. Computer and headphones on.

4 – 8. Work on the phones, Client calls, Email follow up.

8 – 10. Breakfast and Relaxation

10 – 12. Divulge and Edge Work. This is the time when I write and create my blog posts and videos.

12- 2PM Lunch and Meditation

2 – 4. Exercise Time

4 - 6 – Outdoors and Free Time

6 - 8 – Dinner and Varies

That is my Monday through Friday life. I tend to work Saturday morning till 12 Noon, and then I am off until Monday. Sunday is the day in which I don't think about any work related concerns. My mind is allowed to rejuvenate, refresh, and revive.

The last thing I will recommend is that you have a way to manage your thoughts and ideas. If you have too many thoughts running around in your head, you won't be efficient. You will be ineffective. Multi tasking does not work. You can only do one thing at once. Do it and then move on to the next item on your list. To manage my thoughts, I use a web-based program called Simpleology. It is free at the basic level, which is absolutely adequate for most people.

When you have an idea, something to do, or a business idea to explore, or something you might have forgot to tell someone, what do you do? Some people carry around a notebook to write those items down and look at them later. Simpleology works kind of the same way, except it is all digital. I always have my Iphone with me. When I have an idea, I speak to my phone and say "Message to Simpleology." I am then asked for the message. "Explore the idea of an essential oils website." I am then asked if I would like to send. "Send." Tomorrow morning, when I open Simpleology on my laptop, all the items I have texted in will appear in a to do list, which I can edit, prioritize, link to my Google calendar, delegate, create projects, etc. This is not a Simpleology commercial, but it works for me.

I found it invaluable to have a way to keep my mind clean of random ideas. Once I have taken the thought and submitted it into my system, I can then drop it, forget it, all in the knowledge that the idea is safe and waiting for me in the morning when I am in 100% focused work mode. Find a way to manage your mind and thoughts and ideas. Free you mind.

In my case, the way I am wired, I am happiest once I have worked hard and accomplished something. I have a difficult time starting my day with chill time. It doesn't work for me. Some people are night people, and their mornings are all about lounging, and then once the sun goes down, look out. You need to know what type of cycle works best for you and design your day accordingly.

There are a couple of laws I would like to share with you that have helped me to be more efficient with my time and more effective at achieving my results. The first law is called Parkinson's Law. It states: Work expands so as to fill the time available for its completion. In the past, when I had an important project, I would give it a great deal of time. Let's say, for example, I have to write an article for an e-zine. If I allocate 10 hours for the writing of the article, it will take me 10 hours to write the article. However, in fact, of those 10 hours, at most, 2-3 will be spent actually writing, and much of the time will be used inefficiently. Remember the law. Work expands so as to fill the time available for its completion. So instead, I only allocate 4 hours, and those 4 hours are placed right before the deadline, I will be so focused during those 4 hours and produce my best work. No time to dilly dally around. There is an energy around a deadline which you can use to empower yourself to greater accomplishments. Here is another example. I am on a 30-day deadline to write the first draft of this book. Two steps per day in 2 hours of focused writing per day. That is 22 days. The final 8 days are for editing 25 pages per day. Then I will turn it over to someone else for further editing.

The second law is Pearson's Law, which states: That which is measured improves. That which is measured and reported improves exponentially. I keep statistics for many things that I do each day. Pages written. Money earned. Money given away (tips and to the homeless or charity). My weight. Minutes in meditation. I use Simpleology to keep track of these items. This is part of my morning ritual. By measuring the things that are important to me, I remain focused, and I can't go more than a day without realizing when I am veering off course away from my goals. What daily activities would you keep track of? What activities warrant daily observation and reporting? If you say, "I don't know," or, "I don't have any," then I suggest you need to find a bigger game to play so that a few things do matter.

The real beauty of ritual, and incorporating daily discipline to adhere to the activities that most support you in achieving radical freedom, is you also tell your ego, "Hey, you, noisy one, this is how it is going to be, so you might as well take a chill pill and enjoy the ride!"

"As a single footstep will not make a path on the earth, so a single thought will not make a pathway in the mind. To make a deep physical path, we walk again and again. To make a deep mental path, we must think over and over the kind of thoughts we wish to dominate our lives."

—Henry David Thoreau

This is one of my favorite quotes. It is so visual. I imagine walking across a field of tall grass. Each day, step by step, I am carving a path in the earth. With my rituals, day by day, I am incorporating these elements into my life: working, meditating, fueling my body, and luxuriating. Regardless of how my ego may have different ideas, I continue on, and that path I am creating in my mind gets more real and more defined, and I am less likely to get off the path.

Ego is a trickster. Ego is so clever. Ego tells you he or she is your best friend, always there to comfort you when you fall. Beware anything and anyone that pushes you toward comfort and laziness. Ego will do that every time. Ritual will fire you up, day after day. Before you know it, what used to be a challenge simply is a part of your day. No need to worry. No decisions to make. Don't sweat the small stuff. Ritual is your way of saying, "Thanks for sharing, but this is how it's going to be."

Assignment:

What activity in your life warrants being a daily ritual? Exercise? Writing? Creativity? Time with your beloved? Establish a new ritual that absolutely supports your life.

Create your list of vital elements to focus on each day.

Create a daily schedule incorporating those elements.

Develop a system to manage your thoughts and ideas so you don't need to carry any of them around with you.

Execute your plan. Follow your system. Transform your life.

Step 34

Sacred Space

"In monastery darkness
by the light of one flashlight
the old shrine room waits in silence.

While above the door
we see the terrible figure,
fierce eyes demanding. "Will you step through?"

And the old monk leads us,
bent back nudging blackness
prayer beads in the hand that beckons.

We light the butter lamps
and bow, eyes blinking in the
pungent smoke, look up without a word,"

—David Whyte

I first heard these words of poet David Whyte in 2002 at a Grail men's event on Whidbey Island, WA. They are from his brilliant poem, The Faces of Braga. This was the first inkling I had that if I created a sacred space, sacred things may happen. I also felt like I had returned home. Shortly thereafter, I was watching the movie *The Doors* and Jim Morrison (played by Val Kilmer) said something about everybody wanting something sacred in their lives. I found the original context of this comment in an interview:

Jim – "Listen, you two-bit fuckin' actor, you underestimate the audience. You think they all want a better job, a house, two cars, money, that's what you think but you know what they really want, Tom, in their lives, what they really want—"

TOM (Interviewer) - "Tell me.—"

JIM *(a whisper)* "…something sacred, that's what they want, something sacred."

That event, and that poem, and Jim Morrison's words, all pointed me in a direction toward the sacred. The sacred is the special, the ancient, the dignified, and the divine. The sacred is where I go when I meditate. The sacred is where I come from when I am at my best and most authentic self. This step is an invitation to create a space that you can make sacred. This is a first step to having the sacred in your life 24/7. There is richness in a sacred life, and abundance of spirit and guidance, and an undeniable relationship with your higher self. Nothing is taken for granted, nothing and nobody are readily dismissed.

Since 2002, I have had an unquenchable yearning to create and to be in sacred space. I enjoy creating it as much as I do resting in it. Sacred space is not just a place, but a feeling unlike any other. It is a connection to our ancestors. It is an acknowledgement and show of respect for our spirit brethren. For the deeply religious, a church serves as a vessel for sacred space. For others, a long intentional walk through a lush forest inspires the heart. Sacred space creates a unique feeling, a sensation we do not normally experience during our standard day-to-day existence. It feels like we are in a place we do not ever want to leave. With practice, you can forever carry it in your heart, and share it with the world.

Entering sacred space is like entering a new dimension. I often feel I have been transported to an alternate reality. It makes me wonder just how many realities there truly are, and how few of them I even know exist. Time moves differently in sacred space. Sometimes, time moves slowly, and other times, remarkably fast. During meditation, at times

I feel a half hour has elapsed, and yet it has only been a few minutes. Other times, I seem to vanish, and then like a shot, 30 minutes have passed.

So what is the fascination with sacred space? Why create sacred space? What is the objective? What is accomplished? My answer is simple. Creating sacred space is creating a doorway to our deepest truth. Therefore, learning the art of creating sacred space is a skill which may very well contribute to gaining knowledge and experience that will benefit your life. Here are a few time-tested tools you can easily gather and assemble to create a sacred spot in your home:

Candle

Candle holder or bowl

Lighter

Incense

Incense Holder

Silk or special fabric

Sound (Tibetan bell)

That is my complete list. This short list is portable. I can take these items, and sit down virtually anywhere, do a quick set up, and I am transported to sacred space. I will sit on the ground cross-legged, back straight, head slightly downward. The fabric is placed in front of me flat on the ground. I will light the candle first, and then use the candle flame to light the incense, and place each in front of me on the fabric. The last thing I will do is clang the bell to signify the entering into sacred space. I then close me eyes and sit still for 20 to 30 minutes. This is a set up for a meditation session.

Many people find a spot in their home where they won't be disturbed. This will serve as their sacred space, or altar, in which they can place all sorts of sacred objects. If you have a spot like that available for you, wonderful. I have seen some altars with very large pictures of deities on the wall, loads of crystals, candles, incense, and pictures of loved ones. Not everyone has that type of neither space, nor the inclination to feature deities on their walls. For those of us that are more mobile, or space restricted, the set up above serves well.

While sacred space is enhanced with these objects, they are not what create the sacred space. You do. It takes your intention to create the sacred space. Truth be told, you can be in sacred space right now, just by calling it into your life. You are the keeper of your sacred space. You may need all these accouterments to get you started, and get you in the spirit of the sacred, but at the end of the day, you are the vehicle through which the sacred flows. Never forget this. You are sacred, and you may have simply forgotten who you truly are in this moment.

I also use the concept of sacred space for my work life. I have a few sacred objects that I place on my desk. I am constantly burning incense. Incense for me is a pneumonic device. It always puts me in a great frame of mind. Now that I am living in Thailand for a while, I smell incense everywhere, just walking down the street. It is glorious. The smell of incense, a burning candle, and some Gregorian chant on my headphones, and I am ready to sit down, start typing words on my computer, and let the energy flow through me onto the screen.

There are plenty of ways to bring the sacred into your life. Gathering a few items with the intention of creating sacred space is an effective means of calling in the sacred energy. Play around with it, and you will feel it in your heart. Invite the wisdom of the ancients to descend upon you, or rise up from the Earth, and stay open for what happens next. All we can do is invite the sacred among us, and then stay open for visions, and words, and feelings of the divine. One true hit of the sacred and you will never be the same. Your life will be on a whole new trajectory.

Assignment:

Do you want more sacred in your life? If you do, create a space. Make it your own. If any of the items I mentioned move you, use them. Create your temple. Then sit down, close your eyes and feel it.

Step 35

Mystical Sightings

"The way people use the word 'God' is shameless name dropping, that's all. We take too big a step when we conjure up some cosmic intelligence who's supposed to transcend all time and space, then pretend to know him on a first-name basis. Everyone tosses the word 'God' around like they know what it means, but they don't know the first thing. Overuse has drained it of any power it once had. Everybody feels so comfortable with the word, 'God,' they don't feel the need--the necessity--to actually go out and find God. To become God."

—Richard Rose

During my life, I have experienced many and varied mystical experiences. Some experiences are subtle, and some others seemed shocking and unbelievable at the time. It feels important to say that the moments I share here were all experienced without the use of any drugs or ritual medicine. They have all served to alter my experience of life, and have contributed to my understanding of how we experience life.

My first mystical experience occurred during my college days at Cal Berkeley. I was in a philosophy course. I was working at Safeway in the evenings (the night crew) to pay my way. Often I was quite tired in my classes depending on my unit load. I was sitting in class with the professor teaching Descartes' "I think, therefore I am." I began to doze ever so softly and then WHAM! There he was. Jesus, unlike any picture or statue I had ever seen before. He looked at me with the most loving eyes I could imagine. His eyes were olive shaped, wide open, and piercing into me. He also had a crown of thorns, digging deeply into his head, blood flowing down his face. I literally jolted out of my chair and left the class. I didn't know what to do with the experience. I shared it with a few close friends. But more than anything, the experience scared me. I couldn't explain it. I didn't know what it meant. And I felt completely out of control because I didn't ask for it. Apparently I was ready and it happened. Jay, meet Jesus.

In the year 2000, I traveled to England with my family to take a leave from America. As it turned out, my wife and I were asked to help out with a one-week event for which our teacher at the time found himself shorthanded. We had rented a bus, and were prepared to venture out to the English countryside and find crop circles. I was the bus driver.

Now, you would think that my mystical experience would involve crop circles, and the energy of the land, and the meticulous bending of the stems, all of which I leave in the realm of the mystery. This mystical experience happened late one night, somewhere in the middle of the week, while we were all up late. There were about 20 of us in total. We were all staying in an English country house. On this night, I recall sitting back and watching how my teacher interacted with everyone. He had a powerful presence, a magnetism that was undeniable. He was chain-smoking hand rolled cigarettes, and seemed to be in quite a bit of pain, which flared up from time to time. I remember he complained about the celestial heat, and needed to take frequent cold baths to ease the discomfort.

At one memorable moment, my teacher stood up in front of us all, and put his arms out to his side, with his hands at a 45-degree angle to his body. Then he said, "Look at my hands." I looked. And when I looked, I saw white light coming out of his hands, coming out of holes in his hands, all very similar to the holes you'd see in the hands of Jesus. I looked again, and kept seeing the same thing. After a minute, he sat back down, and everything returned to a fairly normal state. My teacher kept saying that he was channeling the Christos energy. He was saying that all week. Later in the week, he pulled me aside, and told me that this house, the house in which we were staying, this was the real sacred site.

I don't know if anyone else saw what I saw. My wife was not in the room at the time. And I was tired, worn out, and simply didn't care if anyone else saw what I saw. At that time in my life, I realized, at a deep place within, that what I had considered "normal" simply was not. My mind expanded to include the unexplainable, the mystical, the psychic, and the magical. With that expansion, which began in earnest on that night in England in 2000, I opened myself up to my own mysticism.

In 2004, I ventured into the evening woods during the fall equinox in Marin County, CA. I noticed how my body wanted to slow down and get quiet. Something much bigger than me was demanding my attention and respect. This sensation became quite strong, especially as I ventured past the lit portion of the forest into the dark and thick quiet. It was profoundly eerie, walking among the huge trees, the moonlight piercing through the rare openings in the canopy, and the subtle sounds of the wind and falling leaves tickling my awareness.

I slowly walked, and utilized the Taoist form of walking, which serves to quiet the body and the mind, allowing me to become more at one with the surroundings. It was quiet, still and beautiful. As I slowed down, I felt myself drawn to the trees, and found myself leaning into one of the larger ones. As I leaned, I felt as if all the tension and anxiousness that was in my body simply oozed out, as if being absorbed by the tree through osmosis. It was decadent beyond words. I had to move to another tree and sit down, my back leaning into this magnificent energy source.

I didn't move for about half an hour or so. I focused my attention on the physical sensations I was experiencing. I listened to the wind. I felt the tree at my back, and the soft ground under my legs. And then I was called to look up, and so I did. And there, in the gap between the trees, I saw the Goddess. She was beautiful, with just her alabaster face looking down at me. I looked up at her for another 10 minutes, listening for her message. And what I heard was, "Even when you don't see me, know that I am always with you." How stunning and glorious! I have since had many such mystical and magical experiences with the Goddess, but this was one of the first, and there is nothing quite like the first. I felt ever so fortunate.

At this point, I realized I had lost track of time, and my friends had headed back out of the forest. So I left my cozy nook next to the tree, and began my trek out of the forest. I noticed how the energy had shifted since I had walked in. The night was darker, the wind louder, and magic was in the air. I opened my eyes and my heart, looking for whatever was next. And she came back to me again.

I was walking and saw her, a woman dressed in white, with a white scarf draped over the front of her. As I approached, she began to fade into the night. Still, I understood we were not through with our interactions. I understood there was still something for me to learn on this night. I went back to my original location and looked at her again, and I watched her. I unfocused my eyes, a technique my teacher had taught me, and I felt for what she was saying to me. She asked me to hug her. Now, I am not one to argue with or question divine guidance. I tried to do things my way in the past, and it didn't work. If I am asked to hug a Goddess, I will do it. It was one of the most heartfelt experiences of my life. She was soft, and she smelled of freshly cut wood. She was glorious to hold. Then, and only then, did I understand the true meaning of her message. "Even when you don't see me, know that I am always with you."

I feel that so much of my work with men had been about connecting our hearts (underused) with our heads (overused). What she was telling me, I believe, is that women have the exact same challenge. Many women are utilizing more of their masculine (their heads) than they really care to. It is survival. There aren't many men around in whose company women can truly relax into their feminine divine essence. There is a disconnect between the Goddess' head and her feeling body. She is screaming to us for the same connection we all strive for, that

12-inch connection between our heart and mind. While I was honored by the wisdom, I also felt a profound sense of mission and purpose, with so many minds and bodies, so rushed, and with so little serenity, stillness, vulnerability and open heartedness.

In 2007, I had just returned from a weekend initiation ritual. I generally return from these types of events fairly opened up. I felt the need for a massage. I had worked hard all weekend, and felt the reward of a massage was warranted. I have an amazing woman named Leslie who usually is my masseuse. She is strong and also gentle and nurturing. Being a massage junkie, I know this combination is hard to find. Leslie fits the bill to perfection.

During this massage, I was graced with the presence of two angels. They were female. They were compassionate. They were divine. I lay on the table with my eyes closed. I opened my eyes and saw two feminine figures hovering over me, approximately 10 feet above me. They were wearing white flowing dresses, with a wind blowing the material gently against their skin. I looked for a while and then closed my eyes. The effects of a great massage are immediate relaxation.

After just another minute, I felt warmth and a slight pressure on my chest. The word warmth does really capture what I felt. If you can remember what it felt like when someone you love tells you they love you, and your heart opens and melts, it was that kind of warmth, to a factor of about ten. As I said, I was really relaxed, but this sensation was so powerful, I had to open my eyes and see what was happening. As I opened my eyes, I was surprised to see both of the goddess angels. They were both laying their head on my chest. I had to catch my breath. I closed my eyes and simply accepted this gift.

Rarely have I ever felt such love as on that massage table. I can remember to this day the exact feeling of that divine grace. I felt such gratitude for the experience. I asked Leslie if she saw them as well. She said she did not, but she felt something special was happening. I told her about the angels and she smiled. It was simply beautiful on so many levels.

Life if full of magic, and as we venture on the path to radical freedom, we open up, and wake up to all the forces and dimensions that surround us. This little chart shows just how little we can see with our eyes. It is remarkable how much more there is going on around us. As we become more aware, the universe seems to reward us with greater insight, perception, and intuitive guidance.

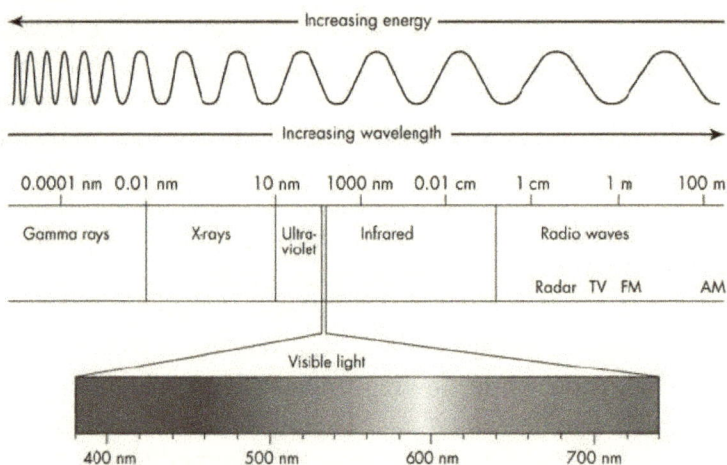

You may feel this is all rubbish. I get that. I use to feel that way. Then I started to see things that defy normal logical explanation. Then I become somewhat adept at creating non-ordinary reality and sharing it with others. This step is an invitation not to believe anything anyone tells you, but to stay open to the possibility that there are many things we don't know that we don't know. In that openness, the world will awaken anew, and that child-like sense of wonder and marvel will start to lift you up and show you the way.

Assignment:

Have you seen something that you can't explain? Don't discount it. Write down the experience to make it real. The more you accept the unexplainable, the more you invite the potent, transformative energy of magic into your life.

Step 36

Gratitude

"Join me in the pure atmosphere of gratitude for life."

—Hafiz

Truth be told, I have not been much of a gratitude guy. The idea of gratitude seemed like a luxury for which I did not have any time. I had to work, be a good husband and father, and keep learning about myself. Gratitude? Why? Who needs it? Well, as it turns out, I need it. When I peeled back all of my own defenses, I came to realize I am very grateful to be alive on this planet at this time. I also realized that when I am in a state of gratitude, my life runs far more efficiently. Gratitude is like the oil of an engine. You can run without it for a while, but things run much smoother with it.

Gratitude requires a bit of humility. Arrogant bastards beware. In order to have authentic gratitude, I must be in a place that acknowledges some sort of higher power, or intelligence, or god, that has all the loose ends covered. The expression of gratitude is implicitly toward someone or something. When I say, "I am grateful for my life!" to whom am I saying this? There is no point in saying it to myself, because I am not the one that had anything to do with having a life. Having gratitude acknowledges that we don't have all the answers, but recognize there is a hidden hand that deserves our appreciation and thanks. Expressing gratitude requires us to surrender to something bigger.

Years ago, my partner asked me, "Where is the gratitude?" My answer was, "I don't have any!" At that time in my life, I wasn't grateful for my health, my wife, my children, my career, my friends, my home, my food, my journey, my awakening, my magic, my gifts, my amazing bullshit detector (do forgive me for rambling a bit here, but it is good medicine), and all the wonderful things I had been blessed with. If you were to look at it on a scorecard, it would read: Gifts – Immense and innumerable. Gratitude – Zip, Nada, No Way, No How. And the scorecard would be read by me with disdain. Like I said, I did not get it. If I were to interpret what the universe was and is saying, it would go something like this: "Hey, Jay, you deaf mute idiot, SNAP OUT OF IT! You are alive. How about a little appreciation?"

Then I thought about it. Doesn't it make simple sense, that if the universe is blessing me with gifts, and I don't seem to give a damn, the universe would stop blessing me altogether? There is the rule. Perhaps the great lesson I will take is that I must take stock of what I have, and dig deep into my heart, all war torn, shell shocked, and unwilling to open. I must have the courage to peel away the clever veneer, and be willing to acknowledge my small little role in this game. And in that acknowledgement of my complete "out of control-ness" I am only left with gratitude for what I have, for it surely wasn't "me" that did it.

This is when I began to learn to slow down. I felt the sun on my face. I felt joy at greeting my family. I marveled at the miracle of my daughter as she worked on a school project, typing away on the MacBook we gifted her for graduation. I really tasted the vanilla frozen yogurt with almonds and chocolate syrup we shared. Gratitude is a courageous searching for humility, awareness, and self-forgiveness. No small task for arrogant bastards such as myself. I am here. I am alive. I am able to do the heavy lifting. And for all that and so much more, I am grateful.

Assignment:

Make a list of no less than 10 things for which you are grateful. In the case of people, follow up by contacting each one and sharing your gratitude. Be sure to tell them the unique gift or quality of theirs for which you are most grateful.

Step 37

Love

"You can search throughout the entire universe for someone who is more deserving of your love and affection than you are yourself, and that person is not to be found anywhere. You yourself, as much as anybody in the entire universe deserve your love and affection."

—Buddha

Love is the law. Love is the truth. Love can be as harsh as it can be beautiful. Therefore, it takes courage to look at your essence in total, for you, at your core, are love. It takes courage to begin the process of knowing yourself. It is easy to look and see all the good stuff. The trick is to look at the dark stuff, come to terms with it, appreciate it, and rather than pretend it doesn't exist, integrate it into your being. In order to truly experience love of any kind, this has to happen. Otherwise your love is a pretend love, the kind that is bandied about in silly love songs. It wears off and does not stand the test of time.

So where do you start? You dive into the hurt. I have never met a human being that did not have some feelings of self-loathing. Often it is self-loathing, like the pain from a persistent pebble in our shoe, which awakens us to action. It's the discomfort that creates the yearning for something greater. It's only in the acquisition of self-knowledge that we begin to appreciate the brilliance of our human condition. It's this appreciation for the universal condition of all beings that begins to look like self-love. But it is not self-love. It is love.

223

Love is not something you direct at yourself or at a chosen other. Love is a state of being, a place you can come from in every moment of your life. In fact, the idea of loving just yourself or just another will, upon ruthless examination, seems nonsensical. When you arrive in life at where you started in life, love is everywhere, like the ticking of the clock in your heart. I love you. This is true. I love me too. You is me. Me is you.

This love, the great love, is available right now. It is in the air we all breathe. It is in the sunlight that warms your skin. It is in the tone of your friend's voice. It is in your lover's breath. You don't need to look for it, for it can't be found. Life calls upon each of us to dive deep within our own being, and in doing so, we begin to clean the lens of our perception. The love is here, more love than we can imagine, the kind of love that has obsessed poets like Neruda and Bukowski and Rumi for lifetimes. It is so powerful, and can be so overwhelming, that we lean back toward what is comfortable, and socially accepted, while the keys to the kingdom of heaven slip out of our hands. Can't you taste it? Are you ready to undertake the hero's quest to unearth the grail? Grab my hand and let's jump into the abyss.

"With love you don't bargain. There, the choice is not yours. Love is a mirror, it reflects only your essence, if you have the courage to look in its face."

—Rumi

The year was 1982.

There was one "I love you" I will never forget, and which unalterably changed my life. Was it from my wife, or a mysterious lover, or an innocent child? No. This "I Love You" was from a woman whose name I cannot now remember.

During my college years at Berkeley, I had two friends who had participated in a two weekend self-improvement workshop call the est training. In those days, the est training had quite a reputation. I remember hearing that you could not go to the bathroom except on infrequent bathroom breaks. This was to demonstrate how your mind can impact matter. Also, something happened to the people who attended the est training, they "got it." I wasn't sure what that meant or what they "got," but according to my friends, it was really important. The folks at the est training also had an effective sales and recruiting program. I attended one guest event, and barely escaped with my money intact.

I was actually quite interested in the est training. Something inside of me was already stirring. And with the recommendation of my two friends, it seemed like a slam-dunk. But as I mentioned, I was raised in a strong Catholic family. This weird California program had the looming stench of religion and cult. For my family, this est business seemed all wrong. They felt very strongly that participating in the est training was going to damage my mind. For many years, I heeded my family's advice and steered clear of the est training. Then I left the nest for good and moved to Chicago.

Relocating to Chicago in 1981 was the first time in my young life I had put some distance between my parents and me. While I had spent 4 years at Berkeley, my parents lived only an hour away from the campus. I returned home on many weekends, and during the summer months. I was also the oldest of three boys, so I believe more attention was placed on me, especially in terms of religious guidance, as I was, in effect, the guinea pig for the next generation Catholic Cradeurs.

But that was old news: now I was away from all of that. I was in Chicago, free to do and be exactly what I wanted to be. While the words of my parents would continue to ring in my ears for many years, each time the sound would be a little bit less forceful. Consequently, I didn't immediately jump into the est training when my plane landed at O'Hare Airport. Instead, my fiancé and I signed up for a different event by the same group, an event called the Communications Workshop. Rather than two weekends, it was one weekend long. It did not have the same reputation as the est training for being so grueling and physically demanding. I had just begun my tenure at my new job at the Leo Burnett Advertising Agency, and thought that a workshop on communications would fit perfectly with my life plans.

I remember walking into the workshop with both excitement and trepidation. I had absolutely no idea what I was walking in to. I guess I must have been 23 years old at the time. Something led me to be at that workshop. Something knew the importance of the workshop on my life. Something had decided that my life would not be my anticipated life of corporate success, mega wealth and CEO stardom.

During the workshop, our leader Linda led us in all sorts of exercises. Most of the time, we were paired up and we would try different things, all in an effort to expose all of the elements of communication. Always relaxed, always with eyes fixed upon each other. The word Intention was used quite often. While now I feel eye gazing is as threatening as my cat's purr, back then I was extremely reserved and self-conscious. Each exercise was an ordeal. I felt challenged at every turn. Gradually throughout the first day, I began to relax and notice I could feel safe in the workshop and begin to enjoy some of these interactions. I also remember being extremely judgmental, and based my satisfaction for an exercise on the quality of my partner. I had absolutely no concept of creating my own reality. I was a pinball bouncing around the bumpers of life.

On our final day, we had the final exercise based on three words: "I love you!" We were asked to say I love you to our partner, nine different ways. I recall we had a grid of three by three to follow. Some of the choices for "I Love You" lacked intention or focus, so we could experience how unsatisfying that felt. However, the final "I love you" was to be said with the maximum intention and focus. My partner was a pleasant and cheerful woman about my age. Totally unexpected, she hit me with the final "I Love You."

That was it.

That was a seminal moment in my young life.

The Earth stopped.

My life began anew. It was like someone had physically injected adrenalin into my heart. My body shivered. Tears came to my eyes. I looked in disbelief at my partner, who had experienced the same sensations, and we were simply in utter bliss, babbling about what we had shared.

I don't remember what happened the rest of the workshop. I was on a high that felt better than any drug I had ever tried, that would last for several weeks. I recall being back at work at Leo Burnett, feeling like the cat that ate the canary. I started to see the world through significantly less clouded eyes. I wondered if there are many others who saw the world this way. I would walk around the building looking deeply into the eyes of all those I met, curious about how present they might be. I was a different person. The reactions of my coworkers were substantial. Clearly something profound was happening to me. It was an Earth shaking discovery to realize that my reality was so limited. If I felt like I felt after a weekend workshop, what else might be available to me in this big beautiful, and up to that point, largely unexamined world.

I wasn't going to achieve mega wealth. I wasn't going to be a titan of industry. No. In that moment, something was exposed to me, something I will never shake. My curiosity and desire then shifted to matters of the heart, to matters of energy and magic, and to matters of the truth. If my name was Ahab, I had found my white whale. A fire was ignited back in Chicago at the Communications Workshop, a fire that I have spent some thirty years feeding.

I now see this moment in others, and wonder how they will fare. The fire is intense, and the results unpredictable. The level of insecurity is often paralyzing. The willingness required to be an obedient servant often seems unreasonable and excessive. You may wonder, why not go back? In my experience, once you feel this kind of unconditional love in your heart, there is no going back. I have seen those that try to forget, or act as if they are all back to normal, and live what author Stuart Wilde calls the "tick tock" life. It doesn't work.

Perhaps love is a strong dose of the sacred. I have come to feel that love is pure consciousness. Therefore, once we can experience consciousness, unfettered by rampant thoughts of survival, and competition, and shame, we can live in a permanent state of love. Love does not require a beloved. It does not even require another person. Create the space, or opening for it to show up, and there it will be. Of all the lies I have believed, my beliefs about love have been the most misdirected, inaccurate, and in need of substantial revision.

Assignment:

If you want to feel the real deal, you have to do the heavy lifting. Invest time into knowing yourself and into understanding who you are through and through. It is as simple as writing your name on a piece of paper, then write "Light Side" on the top left and "Dark Side" on the top right, and begin writing. It's OK to admit to all aspects of yourself, especially to yourself. You will be surprised at the catharsis that occurs when you undertake this simple little process. The purpose of this assignment is to begin the process of loving and accepting all of you.

Step 38

Sweet Surrender

"The older I get, the surer I am that I'm not running the show."

— Leonard Cohen

I am nothing special. In fact, I am nothing at all. This is for me the greatest expression of surrender. To acknowledge the degree to which we have no control of our lives requires a profound surrender. You can get with the program on your own. This is the easier path. Or the universe, as sure as I am writing this, will kick you in the teeth, punch you in the gut, and show you no mercy. If you don't surrender, she will make you surrender! This, for me, is one of the most difficult aspects of the path, the willingness to accept one's true and accurate place in this world.

There is no power that can be owned. There is no gift that can be owned. There is no accomplishment that can be owned. If one is truly to accept the analogy of the hollow bone, how can one feel anything but gratitude for a display of power? Pride and prejudice have no place here. Holding the feeling of "master of the universe" is a sure recipe for a hard fall from grace. When the student is ready, the teacher will appear. One won't be blessed with power until one can be responsible with the power. However, as I look at the world, I don't see this to be the case. Being granted power, as I see it, is a test of the universe to see just where you stand. Blow up and spread your feathers like a peacock, and the power will leave lickety-split. Honor the power, be grateful for the power, share it only when called upon, and more power will be granted. It is that power, treated with respect and honor, which the initiate will need to build the pyramid. It is that power, not owned and claimed as one's own, which will fortify the initiate in the battle with the Great Magician, with himself. It's kind of funny isn't it? It is all an internal battle.

"How are you doing? Good!" "How was your day? Great." It is very subtle, and when you start to really listen, it is everywhere, standing as a part of our human dialogue. How does one break through this falsehood, and begin to realize there can't be good or bad experiences, but only experiences? How does one come to accept that this day is just like the last day, with only one's judgment determining the level of joy or contentment one feels? Waiting in lines is a great example. Seems no one likes to wait in lines, as if they have something so much more important or rewarding to do. I have seen many become so indignant because they had to wait 15 minutes to apply for a driver's license. Why not surrender? Surrender your ego to the universe. You are in line, so why fight it? What is the battle you expect to win? Let it go.

From this one is tempted to break a lance on that most ancient battlefield, free-will and destiny. But even though every man is "determined" so that every action is merely the passive resultant of the sum-total of the forces which have acted upon him from eternity, so that his own Will is only the echo of the Will of the Universe, yet that consciousness of "free-will" is valuable; and if he really understands it as being the partial and individual expression of that internal motion in a Universe whose sum is rest, by so much will he feel that harmony, that totality.

— Aleister Crowley

A friend of mine asked me a question recently about free will. My answer was this… If I am in a boat, floating down the river, and suddenly I see the big boulder in the water that I referred to earlier, what do I do? Well, it seems I have a choice, an opportunity to display my free will. I can either crash into the boulder, or I can row my boat off to the side, and avoid the boulder. Here in lies the illusion of free will, for with either choice, I am going to continue down the river.

The surrender is to life. The surrender is to give up on our false beliefs. The surrender is the act of taming the ego by giving the ego a voice. But you don't need to react to it. Surrender to who you are and to who you are not. I saw a cute cartoon on the Internet. It showed seven animals, a bird, monkey, penguin, elephant, fish, seal and dog. They were lined up for an exam. The teacher, sitting at his desk, says, "For a fair selection, everybody has to take the same exam: Please climb that tree." No matter how hard that fish tries to be a monkey, it's not going to happen. When human beings try to be what they are not, life does not work. Accept your position. Understand your role. Surrender to reality. Embrace how wonderful you do have it.

Assignment:

What do you need to surrender to? Try it out. Surrender. Do like Atlas did and shrug.

Step 39

Acceptance

"In this vastness where will your ego be? In this vastness where will your suffering be? In this vastness where will your mean mind be? The mediocre mind, where will it be? It cannot be there in such vastness, it simply disappears. It can exist only in a narrow field. It can exist only when it is walled, enclosed, encapsulated. The encapsulation is the problem. Live dangerously and be ready to live in insecurity."

—Osho

Who am I to judge? I use to ask myself this question so many times during a day. I had undertaken the process of dismantling all of my beliefs. I realized that any one of my beliefs was more of a hope that something was true. When in reality, if I knew something to be true, it would not be a belief but rather a truth. I further realized that most of my judgments were based on beliefs, or more accurately stated, superstitions, specious thoughts that had no basis in reality. A belief is a lie until I can prove it to be true. As it turned out, I was living with quite a few lies, which were making me a judgmental idiot. I declared in that moment that I would not believe anything.

I have found that the greatest level of acceptance comes from the realization that we really don't know too much for sure. As we have already discussed, this is not something the ego wants to accept. Remember, the ego's biggest enemy is the unknown. Accepting how much we don't know is a tough pill to swallow. What don't you know that you don't know? When you wrap your head around that question, it opens up whole new level of unknown, as well as a healthy dose of humility. We return to … who am I to judge?

You may have been born with the Muslim rulebook, Jewish rulebook, Mormon rulebook, or the atheist rulebook, or the rulebook of no rulebook. Then we heap on top of that the rulebook our parents or guardians impart. Mix in with that the rulebook we share with our friends, as well as the rulebook that governs your country of origin, and you end up with a swarm of beliefs, rules and ways things should be. The idea of returning to the state of a blank slate seems laughable, yet that is what is required to be free of the dogma and religious and social programming.

Is the world flat? Of course not, but had you been born thousands of years earlier, this would have been your reality. They use to believe the sky was a crystal dome from which the stars dangled at night. I could have told you the world is round and the solar system infinite, but 2000 year old you would have thought me crazy. You would have been wrong, but I would have been crazy. What is it that we assume to be true now, that may not be so true? It is something to think about. What don't you know that you don't know?

Now to bring this to daily life, I invite you to ask yourself the question, who am I to judge? We seem to all have this barometer of what is right or wrong, what is good and what is bad. Out of this judgment mechanism, we have racism, sexism, ageism, homophobia and dislike, if not hatred, for just about anyone who is not like us. The other night, I was on Bangla Road in Patong, Thailand, a street famous for just about anything you can imagine sexually. Before their cabaret show, the transsexual women come out and pose for pictures with the tourists walking the street. The ladyboys, as they are called, are men who felt their true essence was that of a woman, and now live their lives as women. I must say, many of them are quite beautiful and feminine and certainly appeared to be right at home in a woman's body.

After having my picture taken, I sat off to the side and watched the proceedings for about an hour. It was fascinating. Most of the tourists would avert eye contact and walk on by. Some were visibly disgusted, as if the ladyboys were deserving of their scorn. And others were accepting, played with the ladyboys as they all posed for pictures. Transsexuals provide us with a great example of a class of people who are judged, criticized and often ostracized because of their sexual identity and sexual preference. We judge them because they are different, because we don't understand them, or somewhere along the path, we developed a belief that who they are or what they do is wrong. I have to say it again, who am I to judge? Well who I am is not better than who anybody else is, so I am going to stop being such a judgmental a-hole and live and let live.

When you accept life (and all its people) on life's term, life takes on a certain ease and flow. When you have established a daily meditation practice, and learn to slow down the thoughts in your head, turn down the volume, and not ascribe too much importance to pre-programmed judgmental thinking, you will go through a glorious transformation in which all of life is exactly as it should be. No resistance is necessary. There is no need to change anything. Everything and everybody is in their perfect place in the world. Can you imagine what it is to walk the earth with this paradigm? How much peace and serenity can you handle?

This is how it is. It always has been. Have you ever done something, or had something done to you, and in the moment, it seemed like it was a big mistake. Yet in the following minutes, hours, days, weeks, months, years, maybe even decades, you can look back and say to yourself something like, "I would never be who I am today if that had not happened." All of the worst things that have happened in my life have also made the biggest contributions to who I am today. Each incident has allowed me to expand my palate of colors. Without these challenges, life would be monochromatic. I did not accept them back then. I accept them now. I find in this knowledge a tremendous freedom to live life unfettered and free. There are no mistakes and life is progressing for all of us in its perfect timing and wisdom.

Accept life just the way it is. Trust life. Trust the process. Trust your intuition. You can't go wrong. Even when it feels like you have gone wrong, you can't go wrong. That's the koan, and time is the great enlightener.

Assignment:

What is there in your life, a person or situation that you either judged harshly, or are unable to accept? What is this position you are taking costing you in your life? How would your life be different if you simply accepted this part of your life for what it is, and not try to change anything? The answer may surprise you.

Step 40

Exuberance

"And in that moment, I swear we were infinite."

— Stephen Chbosky

This step is an invitation to become aware of a unique energy called exuberance. This quote comes from a movie called *The Perks of Being a Wallflower*. This movie presents a trio of characters who are going through their teenage years, just before heading off to college. They are driving a pickup truck through the Fort Pitt tunnels in Pittsburgh. The main character stands up in the back of the truck and raises his arms outstretched. The soundtrack begins playing David Bowie's "Heroes." It captures an exuberant moment, when friends, and the world around, conspire to teach us something and show us a glimmer of how amazing life can be.

I had heard the word exuberance, read it in a book here or there, but never really got it, nor felt it. In my early twenties, I had participated in an est program (est was a two weekend personal development popular in the 1970s and '80s) called the guest seminar leaders program (GSLP). It was an intense 6 month program requiring me to attend several live events each week, attend ongoing training events, and volunteer my time helping out wherever needed. One day I was asked to help to clean Werner Erhard's boat, which was called *Exuberance*. I started to get the energy of the word, and its significance in a life well lived.

My wife and I were assigned to one of the rooms on the boat. We were given all the cleaning tools, and allotted as much time as needed to thoroughly clean the room. We spent the next hour cleaning, and felt we had done an excellent job. We notified our leader, Jack, that we were done. I will never forget his reply. "Already?" He then came into the room with a white glove, and pointed out at least 10 places that he found dust. We learned in that moment what it meant to do a thorough job. Up to that point, I had been the master of the short cut, the quick work around, the easy way to finish. On the boat *Exuberance*, I learned how to do a job with patience and excellence.

Exuberance is defined as being full of energy, of being ebullient, of growing profusely. It is a telltale sign that you are on a path toward radical freedom. I have often felt exuberance while reading a book. I remember reading Carlos Castaneda's book *The Teachings of Don Juan* and feeling so full of energy, life, and expectancy. I was exuberant as I realized I had discovered wisdom that spoke to me, and inspired me, and at some level, woke me up. I also felt this way reading Stuart Wilde's books, particularly *The Whispering Winds of Change*. He spoke about fringe dwellers, and I realized that someone else knew exactly how I felt. Ten years ago, I read the first of the three Jed McKenna books, *Spiritual Enlightenment, The Damnedest Thing*. I was lit on fire. I stayed up all night reading that book. At last, I had found someone who could speak to my own experiences. That was a 24-hour period of pure exuberance.

Do you want to feel more exuberance in your life? One way is to burn the boats. Burn the boats is an expression used to describe the act of taking on a challenge, and not leaving yourself any option, save to move forward. A famous Spanish conquistador, Hernan Cortes, landed on the shore of Mexico in 1519. He did not have enough men, or artillery, or training to realistically have a chance to overthrow the Mexicans and lay claim to their land and treasures. Cortes gathered his men, gave an inspiring speech, and then shouted out his final order: "Burn the boats." He eliminated the option of retreat. It was either going to be victory or death. He filled each man with exuberance, a chest full of energy, all poised to move in only one direction. As the story goes, Cortes and his men did, for the first time in 600 years, conquer Mexico.

What makes you feel exuberant? This will help guide you in a direction that is true. When you find something you can do that feels exuberant, you will most likely succeed. Love what you do, and do what you love. For the longest time, I had not even asked myself the question of what filled me with energy. I did what I did, and I wasn't ever exuberant. I worked a job like so many. It wasn't until I started to feel exuberant through books that I realized how much I enjoyed writing and talking about things that mattered to me. I am exuberant when I am radically free.

Assignment:

What can you do today that will have you feel exuberant? Go do it.

Step 41

Awakening

"Enlightenment is a destructive process. It has nothing to do with becoming better or being happier. Enlightenment is the crumbling away of untruth. It's seeing through the facade of pretense. It's the complete eradication of everything we imagined to be true."

—Adyashanti

There is a profound beauty inherent in every moment. It is an aching awareness, an excruciatingly profound knowing that this life, this experience, right now, is precious. The more you slow things down and find that still center in the heart of your being, the more you will come to experience life on life's terms. Therein lies the gorgeous beauty of our existence. When you get beyond the celebrations, the self-congratulations, and the extravagances, there you may find the mountainous presence of this exact moment. It is so subtle, and yet not. When you feel it, you will be forever changed.

Life is not an experience to be dominated. Rather, it is a dance, a romantic give and take, a love affair with the unknown. Life, which I'll refer to as She, has so much to offer. We are called upon to be receptive and open to attract Her precious gifts: love, bliss, grace, connection, and the incredible self-knowledge that no matter what happens, life has your back. There is a freedom to letting it all go, and allowing the white rapids of life to show you exactly who and what you are in a way that will wash away all fears and concerns.

"If you're brave enough to leave behind everything familiar and comforting, which can be anything from your house to bitter, old resentments, and set out on a truth-seeking journey, either externally or internally, and if you are truly willing to regard everything that happens to you on that journey as a clue and if you accept everyone you meet along the way as a teacher and if you are prepared, most of all, to face and forgive some very difficult realities about yourself, then the truth will not be withheld from you."

—Elizabeth Gilbert

Life is patiently waiting. Life has always been waiting. One day you will jump. It is inevitable; for that is the way the river flows. When you are ready, you will show up. It starts by getting honest about the role you play in your life. It starts by eating some humble pie, and acknowledging the precarious nature of our existence. It starts by surrendering to life, and thereby getting into greater alignment with life. She will forge a partnership that has an unbreakable bond. In this partnership, you get out of the way and allow life, in all her power and glory, to work through you. It's a tacit agreement that you will serve as a conduit, fully aware that your gifts and accomplishments truly are not your own.

She calls upon us to be vulnerable, soft, willing, and purposefully aware. Then the dance will begin in earnest, the dance of life that starts with one conscious breath. These are life's terms. This is life's promise to you. The invitation to awaken remains at your doorstep.

Enlightenment happens in a moment. This may be true, but also misleading. The truth that few own up to is this: It takes years, if not lifetimes, of ruthless unearthing of the false self, a dogged determination to know thyself, and a willingness to let go of the self you think you are, all in order to crawl, beaten and broken, to the precipice of a powerfully remarkable and rare occurrence. Then, and only then, and only accompanied by grace, the final transformation requires a heroic, heretofore unrecognized courage and blind exuberance, to make that leap from which you will never return. You will transcend this reality.

Then you may say you gave up everything to be nothing.

"Life has no meaning a priori... It is up to you to give it a meaning, and value is nothing but the meaning that you choose."

— Jean-Paul Sartre

Life is empty and meaningless. It is we the people who assign to it all meaning and significance. Jean Paul Sartre was the first to state out loud that we are a blank slate. We are the artists of our own creative palate of life. Our goal is to get to the point where all beliefs, assumptions, and social conditioning fall away. This is a powerful shift in context, from tarnished to virginal. All we are is an opening for life to show up. This is another way of expressing the Native American metaphor of the hollow bone.

All of this is wonderful for us in two profound ways. First, we know such a moment of awakening, of the ultimate freedom, is available for us all. What one man can do, another can do. Second, if you accept (or at least understand the concept) that meaninglessness and emptiness is our natural state, our always present blank slate, then we all have the ability and unmitigated privilege to create any life we desire. Life is an immense white canvas, and we have the big box of 64 crayons. Color on, one and all. Anything is possible once we clear the clutter of our mind. This is the golden path. This is the holy journey. This is the ultimate undertaking for which we have arrived here and now in this place. Game on.

Assignment:

What is a powerful realization you have experienced? When did the way you see life shift? When did the clutter of your mind lighten up and you had a profound moment of clarity?

Step 42

No Regrets

"Be sorry for nothing."

—Joe Black

This quote is from one of my favorite movies, *Meet Joe Black*. Brad Pitt plays Joe Black, death in human form, come to take away Bill, played by Anthony Hopkins. Joe and Bill's daughter Susan fall in love. Joe is visiting at the hospital where she works as a doctor. She said something factually incorrect, and then says, "Sorry," like so many people do, almost like asking for permission to be alive. That is when Joe says, "Be sorry for nothing." In other words, isn't life too short to be feeling sorry for things that hardly matter in our lives? There really is no book of "shoulds," as in you should do this or you should do that. As we say in our household, stop should-ing all over yourself! Its messy and a waste of time.

We all want to know that this life we lived meant something. We will want the stories, the conquests, the challenges and the success. We will want a fullness and breadth of all that life has to offer. We all want to sit on our deathbed one day and look back and not have any regrets. We will want those memories of crazy powerful love, unbridled passion, and openhearted connections with those special people in our lives. I don't think any of us are going to look back and fondly remember the job we got, the money in our bank account, the car we purchased, the way we played it safe, or the love we let slip away. It must be heartbreaking to look back and wonder where all those years went,

245

and wonder what the hell were you thinking!

This step is an invitation to look at your life and determine what matters to you and what does not. This is an invitation to let go. Surrender. Stop fighting life. I have had to admit to my arrogance and pride. I have stopped trying to control everything. I have stopped listening to what others tell me as they argue for mediocrity. Go with the flow. Don't think you know how any of this turns out. All of this requires courage, for we are embracing the unknown. Fear is lurking just around the corner. The fear is your ego all dressed up and ready to play. Go tell him to piss off once and for all, and see how that works.

I have been thinking quite a bit lately about how I live my life, and what is truly important. I have been putting things into the perspective of, "If I knew I only had 6 months to live, would I look back in 6 months and have any regrets?" I know I sure do take the future for granted, like it is definitely going to be there when I am ready. When men attend one of my weekend events, they are given the opportunity to participate is a life affirming ritual in which they confront their own mortality. If this were my last day, how has my life in totality been? What was really important, and what was more or less bullshit? Where did I waste time? Did I spend my time with people that mattered to me? Did I live honorably? Does that matter? In the end, what will I regret? In the end, what will I remember and say, "I am so happy that I did that!" or, "I can't believe I let that opportunity pass me by!" It makes me ponder the questions of what is a life well lived. In the end, I choose radical freedom.

Radical freedom demands that I remove all the filters that I have placed in front of my eyes, so that I may see clearly and without blind spots. What does it mean to be unfiltered? For me, it means being vulnerable. It means being open. It means living unprotected. It means going for it 100%. As one of my friends would say, it means sharing brave open love. It means not always having it figured out. It means daring to let go. It means lightening up. It means accepting and not controlling. It means going against most everything I was taught about protecting myself and not getting hurt. It means living in a space most people stay away from, and being okay with it.

It also means feeling the real depths of love, rather than the mediocrity of convenience. It means living as a true adult, putting aside my teenage ways of being. What is the point of being here in physical form on this amazing planet if I am not willing to feel and breathe in the true depth of the experience? Being that my horoscope sign is cancer, and we cancer folk are supposed to be highly sensitive, I feel things rather profoundly. I have known the lacerations of betrayal. I have felt such joy with my children. The disappointment of expectations unmet and love lost has brought me to tears.

"The world is a wonderfully weird place, consensual reality is significantly flawed, no institution can be trusted, certainty is a mirage, security a delusion, and the tyranny of the dull mind forever threatens — but our lives are not as limited as we think they are, all things are possible, laughter is holier than piety, freedom is sweeter than fame, and in the end it's love and love alone that really matters."

— Tom Robbins

I am so happy to include a Tom Robbins quote. He wrote one of my all time favorite books, *Jitterbug Perfume*. Love is a unique energy. Lately, I have learned to ride the wave of this energy. It is very attractive. It is big and it is intoxicating. I have learned to swim in it. I notice how both men and women are drawn to it. It is irresistible. There is fearlessness necessary for the real thing to appear, else it is all pretense and that is very unattractive. Love is a current. It is not an agreement. It is not an arrangement of, "I will love you if you love me back." That is not living unfiltered. Rather, that is living protected. That is not being vulnerable. That is hedging my bets. It is not courageous. It is not living at my edge. Living out loud takes me to the places of courage, willingness, release, surrender, forgiveness, adoration, devotion, peace, joy, and returning to source. None of this is possible in a protected state. Vulnerability is the key. Security, while not exactly the enemy, will make your travails on this journey very challenging and often painful. What will you regret?

247

Do you want to know what the 5 biggest regrets are for the dying? Bonnie Ware, an Australian nurse who provides palliative care for dying patients, has recorded their most common regrets. One of the top ones is "I wish I hadn't worked so hard." What would your biggest regret be if this was your last day of life?

Here are the top five regrets of the dying, as witnessed by Ware:

1. I wish I'd had the courage to live a life true to myself, not the life others expected of me.

2. I wish I hadn't worked so hard.

3. I wish I'd had the courage to express my feelings.

4. I wish I had stayed in touch with my friends.

5. I wish that I had let myself be happier.

Helen Keller said, "Life is either a daring adventure or nothing." Which is it going to be for you? Do you know that the universe will always only give you what you can handle? Can you rest in the knowing that you are being watched over, and being held safe and warm? After a bad day, then comes a truly magnificent and miraculous day. As Michael Franti wrote in his song "Yes I Will," "When you're lost and alone, that's when a rainbow comes." Today is a day to let go of the past, and embrace what is showing up for you now. Give your light new places to shine. If I died tomorrow, I will know I did not play it safe and protected. I opened my soul, shared all I have, and loved like a true heart warrior. No Regrets!

Assignment:

For each of the five items, create an action item that will most assuage the regret. For example, #3, to whom do you need to express your feelings? Go do it.

Step 43

Live In Infinity

"If the doors of perception were cleansed every thing would appear to man as it is, Infinite. For man has closed himself up, till he sees all things thro' narrow chinks of his cavern."

— William Blake

A re you infinite? Do you have any sense that you existed before birth, and will continue on after death? I do. I am not sure how exactly I arrived at this feeling. I was reading a book called *The Initiate* written by His Pupil. I picked up this odd green colored book at a garage sale. The wisdom in the book was astonishing for me at the time some 15 years ago. *The Initiate* kept telling the pupil he needed to experience his life in terms of infinity. These words, along with my experiences in meditation, and during various spiritual journeys all left me with the comforting feeling that this gig as a speck of consciousness is a permanent one. Suddenly, worrying about who loves me and who doesn't love me all became background noise from the bleachers in my life.

Living in infinity freed me up from stress. The fear of not surviving suddenly became moot. Strong feelings I may have for someone did not demand any immediate action. My spirit is infinite, and I will be around forever. The first law of thermodynamics states that energy is conserved; it can neither be created nor destroyed, just changed from one form to another.

This conversation leaves me curious about what others have said on the topic. Here are a few quotes you might find helpful.

"Meditation is the dissolution of thoughts in Eternal awareness or Pure consciousness without objectification, knowing without thinking, merging finitude in infinity."

—Voltaire

"I have all the time in the world. I am in touch with the timeless. I am surrounded by infinity. When I think like that, it doesn't mean I'm going to miss my train, it just means that I'm not thinking about it right now because I'm speaking to you."

—Deepak Chopra

"Nay verily, as all joy coming from without is conditional, so all Bliss coming from within is unconditional, and hence eternally present whether we know it or not. And yet, even the joy which as I have said comes from without, does so in appearance only, and not in reality, for neither wealth nor lands, nor delicious food, nor gorgeous apparel contain joy in themselves, but only serve to draw out a minute portion of that infinite joy latent in the soul of every being. "

— The Initiate

The idea that you are infinite, and that your existence is infinite, and that you can feel the infinite in yourself and in everything and everybody is a real stretch for the ego to get behind and support. Getting to the place where you know you are infinite takes some work, and some trickery, and some surrendering of the tiller in your life. So the first step is to understand and accept the concept of infinity on a logical level. You can begin with, "I am infinite, I was around before birth, and will be around after death." You don't even have to believe it, but try it on for size. Stay open for the possibility that this is absolutely true. Allow your ego to have its doubts, but also keep the option open.

If you take action on even a few of the steps in the book, you will begin to notice your feelings of being infinite will grow and expand. It is the feeling that you can not deny. Once you feel your infinite nature, then you will have it locked in. You will feel the infinite nature of all existence. You will feel a part of everything and everyone. Your life will take on an ease and grace as you settle into your infinite nature. My first true feeling of being infinite came from reading a book. That feeling exploded in me during my Samadhi experience at Salmon Creek Beach in Bodega Bay 10 years ago. As you have similar experiences, you won't need any logical explanations. You will know, without a doubt, that you are not a body walking the Earth, but an infinite spirit that is here for a visit before continuing on to the next place.

This path is tough. Some of the steps in this book require such courage and determination and surrender that many will settle for the status quo, and live what will be a perfectly acceptable and lovely life. As I said in the beginning, this book is for those of us who feel there is something more, something powerful and glorious, which is calling upon us to find the truth that lives within us. Exuberance is not found in the status quo. Someone may get excited about purchasing a new car, or earning a job promotion, but that joy will be short-lived, as there will always be a better car to buy and a higher paying job to get. Conditional existence just can't be satisfying. Radical freedom, living in the sacred, honoring who you are, these are the things that consistently deliver. Once you experience your infinite nature, the world will never be the same.

Assignment:

Have you had a moment when you felt infinite? Write the moment down to make it real. Also, ponder on having an infinite nature. In other words, if you are infinite, how would that change how you experience your life right now? How might that impact your fear of death?

Step 44

Radical Freedom

"If you want to find the secrets of the universe, think in terms of energy, frequency and vibration."

—Nikola Tesla

This journey starts with you. The word selfish has acquired a bad name. Still, I am asking you, from this day forward, to be selfish. By that, I am asking you to put you first. Take care of yourself first. Treat yourself well. Invest time and energy into your personal development. This book is an attempt to lay out some steps you can take with you along your journey. The steps each offer you a different look at how you might achieve radical freedom, which is ultimately learning who you are and then being true to who you are.

It all comes back to you figuring out how best to manage yourself to get what you want out of life. This book focused on things you can do today to start strengthening your self, to start raising your energy, to start developing your gifts so you have something of value to share. What you will soon realize is that all you have is your story and your unique way of expressing it. You have a story, a life that has gotten you to this point. You must embrace your story, be generous with your story, and regardless of your feelings of fear, shout it out from the mountaintops.

I believe each one of us is on a true hero's journey. We found ourselves on planet Earth, and we each have endured some ridiculously difficult times. No one has it easy, and no one is getting out of here alive. Unfortunately, the vast majority of people don't really get that this is all coming to an end. Stop playing it safe. Figure out your gifts. Craft your story. Get over yourself and start to live like there is no tomorrow. You have something to share. You have something to say. You have something the world is waiting to hear. You are infinite, so what do you have to lose?

This next section presents 8 discernible stages in the process of achieving radical freedom. Not everyone goes through all the steps, and they don't always happen in the same order. I present these as a guideline, or a set of markers, for someone to gauge where they may be, and where they are going.

1 – Budding Awareness.

There comes a time when we feel that something doesn't ring true. For all of our life, we have been given information. We have been told how to behave, how to function in society, and what to believe. The key phrase for this phase is, "Things aren't what they seem." Another way to put it is, "The story I have been told does not ring true." During this phase, there is a spark of excitement. It is our true nature to be free of all false notions and beliefs, and during this phase, we begin the process of exploring and understanding our true nature, and that is very stimulating. The degree of our desire and curiosity from this point forward will determine just how fast we move to the ultimate clarity and freedom that awaits us all.

2 – The Noise.

Once the excitement dies down, we return to our current state of being. While our awareness has expanded to notice things are not what they seem, and perhaps the way we have been experiencing our whole life is shifting, our awareness in other areas also increases. Most noticeably, it starts to get a bit louder in our head. Throughout this whole process, we will be butting heads with our ego. We are not out to kill the ego, for we need the ego to survive. Rather, we are going to learn to tame the ego, quiet the ego, and understand all the complexities of the ego. Your greater awareness triggers a danger signal to the ego. In order for the ego to survive and thrive, it prefers us to stay asleep, with little awareness, and little desire and curiosity about another way of being. The increase in the volume is a key component of the process, for it serves to amplify our desire and curiosity to find an alternative way to be in this world. Essentially we have begun a civil war inside our being, and it begins to cry for a solution.

3 – Recognize the Dynamic

We don't like the noise. It is naturally offensive to our true nature. Therefore, the noise drives us to assess the situation, identify the noise, and understand the motives of the ego. We are driven to find a way to quiet the noise. The noise informs us to recognize that there is a specific dynamic we must understand in order to experience peace. This dynamic is the relationship between the false self and the true self. It is the dynamic between the actor in the play, and the observer of the play. As long as we think we are the actor, there will be noise. This recognition is at first quite shocking. Lives are lived with the false belief that we are one, when in fact, we are two. This recognition of the dynamics of our basic nature is fundamental to our health, our prosperity, and our clarity.

4. Be the Observer.

Not until we begin to experience ourselves truly as the observer will there be any true peace in our lives. For many, the practice of meditation allows for the experience of oneself as observer. Until we can sit in our truth as the observer of everything, we will always be struggling to honor the demands and the desires of the actor, of the ego. You can't eat enough, have sex enough, make enough money, or have enough of anything to achieve peace and clarity and serenity. There is always more, or another, or something more interesting, yet a shinier piece, and on and on it goes. This is the stage where one begins in earnest to understand the nature of his or her being. With this stage, curiosity and desire for the ultimate awakening are bolstered. Exuberance explodes from within. Power is discovered in the silence. Life is starting to feel more real. You are beginning to experience yourself as the infinite center.

5 – Energy and Intuition Emerge

This new framework is like a crack in the cosmic egg. There is a whole new realm of awareness that is descending upon you. Life begins to make sense in a different way. The old way of being simply won't do. Life begins to be experienced in terms of energy and intuition. It is kind of like you have been given a new operating system. It's an upgrade that makes the old ways of operating obsolete. The prism through which you have experienced your life is cleansed and expanded. Life is less calculated and based more on feelings. Somebody walks into your life, and you feel who they are, rather than taking much stock in their resume. Your inner voice, when it does speak to you, is in the form of intuition. You are better equipped to recognize it and trust it and act in alignment with it. It takes some getting used to, but it works much better.

6. Synchronicity.

This is the beginning of the period of miracles and perfect divine timing. As we continue to open up to a new world, which we don't fully understand, the act of staying open, of surrendering, of letting go, creates a space for what looks like extraordinary events. You think of someone, and then they call you on the phone. You need $200 and somehow it shows up unexpectedly. A friend delivers the perfect book for you to read. You may not see angels like I did, but you will have your own experiences that serve to strengthen you and make you more solid in this new way of being in the world. Old wounds begin to lighten and heal. Life becomes a more relaxed experience. Your opinions don't seem so important. In fact, you wonder why you even have opinions since everything seems to be working out A-OK without any tampering on your part. The magic of life makes itself present.

7. Supreme Clarity

Something happens. It happens. It may be big and bold and beautiful, as I shared about my beach experience, or it may be subtle, without much fanfare. It may be called Samadhi. It may be a final recognition of an awakening. Regardless, you know something happened. You know that a big something happened. You know you will never be the same. It may feel like divinity. It may feel like grace. It may feel like infinity. Words fail to convey the significance of a lifetime's work coming to fruition. One begins for the first time to feel his or her true nature devoid of ego's constant tampering.

8. Radical Freedom

Having a moment is not full awakening. Once your ego gets a whiff of what is happening, it will, hand in hand with Maya, the goddess of illusion, begin to tempt you and work to lure you back to sleep. This is the step that will make you crazy. You will be riddled with questions and self-doubt. Hold strong. This is the time to focus all your energy on the task at hand. Stay the course. Many get to this point, and then stop, thinking they have finished. If only it were that easy.

Once the awareness is abiding and not temporary, then a permanent clarity is achieved. There will be no need to change the world. There will be no need to change anyone. The world will appear as the perfect creation that it is. The need to fix anything will evaporate in the wisdom of your true nature. This is a period of great transition and adjustment. One cannot prepare for the impact of the blinding clarity. Learning how to function in the world after achieving this state takes time. Be gentle with yourself and experience the spaciousness of it all. It is a time for patience. It is a time to let the mud settle so that the water may remain clear. It is time to be radically free.

"The ego is the greatest obstacle on your path towards the Truth. The ego has no real existence of its own, for the mind and the ego are false. At present we are under the impression that the mind and ego are our friends, but they are only misleading us, taking us away from our true nature. Not only do they

delude us, they also cover the face of our real nature. Know this and try to come out of the limited shell of your mind and ego. The seedling cannot emerge and grow into a large tree unless the outer shell breaks and dies. Likewise, the inner Truth cannot be realized, unless the ego dies.

—Mother Amma

Final Assignment:

Go be a radical!!

Final Words

so much depends

upon

a red wheel

barrow

glazed with rain

water

beside the white

chickens.

—William Carlos Williams

I first heard this poem in an English class I took at UC Berkeley. Why, you ask, would I select this short poem for my final words? When I heard this poem, and the ensuing discussion about its merits and imagery, I, for the first time, fell in love with words. Words, with their power to evoke feelings, and mental images, and visceral reactions, became a seminal part of my life. I began writing love poems, and then articles, and essays, and ultimately, blog posts and books.

So much of what I write about defies logic and accurate description through words. We do our best with what we have. Some experiences, however, you can't really get through words unless you have had a similar experience. Describe riding a bike to someone who hasn't, and they won't ever get it until they mount the bike and give it a go. So, I suppose much of my life has been about giving it a go.

Most all of my heroes wrote books. I respect the lonely times, the uninspired moments, and the commitment to share an experience, a journey, or a simple, elegantly detailed story. Painter Chuck Close spoke up on the Charlie Rose show, laughing as he said, "Inspiration is for amateurs, the rest of us show up and get to work!" When I heard those words, I felt like someone had punched me in the gut. "Inspiration is for amateurs." In other words, create the space for the magic to show up. Exercise discipline. Create the space, day after day; put my fingers on the keyboard, day after day, regardless of my feelings. Inspiration is for amateurs! So here I type.

Thank you, dear reader. I trust something was communicated, an idea resonated, a feeling reverberated or a new rung on the ladder was climbed. In the end, I only have my story, and these words are my attempt to share an adventure with a reader.

Finally, I heard someone say that everyone has one book in them. Not many people have two. Book number two is now officially underway. What will spirit bring? I remain grateful and in your service.

www.ingramcontent.com/pod-product-compliance
Lightning Source LLC
Chambersburg PA
CBHW021355090426
42742CB00009B/859